CREATING
AN
ACCESSORY
APARTMENT

CREATING
AN
ACCESSORY APARTMENT

Patrick H. Hare
Jolene N. Ostler

Illustrations by Hattie H. Hartman

McGraw-Hill Book Company

New York   St. Louis   San Francisco
Toronto   Hamburg   Mexico

1 2 3 4 5 6 7 8 9 D O C D O C 8 7 6

ISBN 0-07-026087-7

LIBRARY OF CONGRESS CATALOGING-IN-PUBLICATION DATA

Hare, Patrick H.
  Creating an accessory apartment.

  Includes index.
  1. Housing, Single family—United States—Conversion
to accessory apartments.   2. Accessory apartments—
United States.   I. Ostler, Jolene N.   II. Title.
HD7287.6.U5H33 1987   643'.2   86-20179
ISBN 0-07-026087-7

BOOK DESIGN BY PATRICE FODERO

CONTENTS

ACKNOWLEDGMENTS

Any book of this type draws on the resources of many people. Many are mentioned in the text. Some are not. Among the many whom it is a pleasure to remember for their support and technical assistance is Margaret Haske, a gerontologist, who drafted the chapter on services exchanges and is Patrick Hare's wife. Barbara Foresti and Dee Snowden of the Montgomery County, Maryland, Office of Landlord and Tenant Affairs provided a great deal of assistance on the permit process and on leases. Dennis Day-Lower and Leah Dobkin, director and former education director of the National Shared Housing Resource Center, contributed a great deal, both directly and indirectly, to the chapters on services exhanges. Over the past three or four years they have taught us a great deal about how unrelated people can live together well. They have also become our good friends.

Deborah Stein, an architect, who ran the country's first program on installing accessory apartments, contributed numerous insights to this book both personally and through her writing. Any homeowner in the San Francisco area who is thinking of installing an accessory apartment would be wise to contact her for assistance. Her address is Deborah Stein,

414 Lee Street, Oakland, CA 94610, and her phone number is (415) 835-8824.

We also owe a great deal to Doreen Bierbrier of the Housing Connection in Alexandria, Virginia, for her insights and humor. William Reed, a Washington, D.C., architect, gave us help with construction costs, as did Robert Hare, Patrick Hare's brother and a sculptor and cabinetmaker in Kingston, New York. Roger Burke, Patrick Hare's brother-in-law and a builder in Ipswich, Massachusetts, also provided assistance on production costs. And there are many others.

It is also necessary to give thanks to people who provided support and friendship throughout Patrick Hare's long interest in accessory apartments. There are too many to mention, but particular thanks go to Leo Baldwin, formerly Housing Coordinator for the American Association of Retired Persons, now head of Leo, Inc., of Washington, D.C. Thanks also go to Linda Hollis, a former associate. Finally, we would like to thank Lisa Frost of McGraw-Hill for her editorial assistance and for being so pleasant under pressure.

INTRODUCTION

An accessory apartment is a separate, complete, and independent living unit typically created from the surplus space in a single-family home.

Who can benefit from an accessory apartment? If you are a young homebuyer, the rental income from an apartment can help you carry mortgage payments on the home you really want, rather than a starter home. If you are an empty nester, an accessory apartment can mean extra income, and extra security for your house while you are on vacation. If you are an older homeowner, it can mean money to pay for needed services, and added security from criminal intrusion and accidents when alone. If you are a single parent, suddenly divorced or widowed, it can mean enough extra income to hang on to the family home so that your kids don't lose a parent and a neighborhood at the same time. If you are the adult child of an aging parent, it can mean a way to provide support while still preserving independence.

There are others who can benefit from an accessory apartment. The groups listed above are only the most obvious ones. This book is written to be of use to as broad an audience as possible, from single parents to older homeowners, and from empty nesters to young homebuyers. No matter how the apartment is going to be used, the process of installing it and the considerations that go into deciding to install it, are the same for most people.

The basic premise of this book is that you can take a house that has more space than you want and make the extra space provide you with things that you have less of than you want—income, added security, and services. It is a book about how to install a rental apartment in a single-family house in order to make your life better.

In that sense, it is a book about a new American dream and how you can make it work for you. Not the dream of the postwar years, of the fifties and sixties, of a single-family house in a new neighborhood, but a dream for today's realities.

No one promotes the dream. Occasionally there are articles in magazines such as *Better Homes and Gardens* and *Family Circle*. But there are no ads in magazines for accessory apartments and no commercials on TV implying that accessory apartments, like soft drinks, "are it." No one is going to make enough money off them to afford that kind of promotion, or at least no major companies are.

The people who will do well out of accessory apartments are not major companies but individual homeowners. They are people who have extra space in their homes. Not all homes have room for accessory apartments. Not all homes that have room are designed so you can put an apartment in them. But if you can install one in your home, you will have more money to spend. You may also have a way to get services you need by offering a reduction in rent in return for the services. You will have added security in your home, and you may have added companionship if you and your tenant want it. And finally, you will have provided housing that is needed by others.

Installing an accessory apartment in a home is not a simple job for most people. The purpose of this book is to make it as simple as possible. It builds on work done by others, as others will build on it. A book like this cannot cover everything; however, to the extent possible, this book covers everything you will need to know.

The book is organized to give the reader a feeling for the problems and benefits of installing an accessory apartment. The first two chapters, "Is an Accessory Apartment for You—Some Basic Questions and Answers" and "How to Think About It," provide the overview, without the detail. The chapters that follow repeat some of the material covered in these first two chapters but add a great deal more detail, fleshing out that overview.

Where necessary, references are given to other books or to other ways to get information. When the references are to books that should be available from local libraries or bookstores, just the author and title are given. Where references are made to books or other materials that are not easily available, or are uniquely valuable, full information on how to get the material is given.

Finally, a note should be made about the way in which we have referred to tenants. Tenants can be men or women or mixed groups, families with children or single parents with children. It would be awkward to say "he, she, or they" in order to include all these possibilities every time a reference is made to a tenant or tenants. To avoid this problem, we generally refer to a "tenant" even though it would be more correct to say "tenant or tenants."

In 1982 one of the authors of this book, Patrick Hare, was the director of a study of homeowners and tenants in accessory apartments that was carried out for the Andrus Foundation of the American Association of Retired Persons. Eighty-seven homeowners who had accessory apartments were interviewed. Of those, 73 percent were very satisfied with how the apartment had worked out, 24 percent were satisfied, and only 3 percent were dissatisfied. The results of the study were a clear endorsement of accessory apartments by people who had them in their homes. The benefits they received, including income, added security, companionship, and services, can also be yours. This book can show you how to get them.

CHAPTER 1

IS AN ACCESSORY APARTMENT FOR YOU?

Some Basic Questions and Answers

The main reason people install apartments is for extra income. Besides the extra income, however, accessory apartments can also offer other prospects of comfort and security for homeowners. People living alone may be reassured by having someone else in the house—without giving up privacy, since the privacy of both households is assured. A homebound individual can seek out tenants to provide companionship or occasional transportation. In fact, in return for a reduction in rent, that extra space can provide a homeowner with shopping assistance, baby-sitting, household repairs, and many other benefits and services.

The following questions and answers are intended to help get you started thinking about an accessory apartment. Reading them, you may end up with more questions than answers. Don't be dismayed. The same material is covered again in more detail later. Also, some of the questions may not directly address your concerns. If you are an older homeowner, you may not be interested in how an accessory apartment can help single parents. Feel free to skip questions that don't relate to you.

Why is surplus space worth so much?

There is a tremendous housing shortage in most areas of the United States today, and it is particularly acute for small, reasonably priced rental units. Baby boomers are now setting up homes of their own, so there are simply more small households seeking shelter than in the past. Also, many more people live alone than ever before: students, young people between school and marriage, and divorced and widowed people. Young people are deferring marriage and childbearing until their thirties and are then having fewer children than in the past. Divorce is breaking families into two small households both seeking shelter. Finally, people live longer today and remain in homes that previously would have been released to younger people.

While the need for housing is rising, construction of new homes and apartments has been declining due to high building costs. Condominium conversion has taken large numbers of rental units off the market. Together these two trends have made rental apartments scarce and are driving rents sky-high. In many areas, even people who can pay simply cannot get desirable living accommodations.

So . . . whoever has an apartment to rent has a great deal of bargaining power in this country.

If accessory apartments are such a great idea, then why haven't they caught on before now?

They have. Many owners have rental units in their homes. Open the newspaper to the rental housing ads and you will see them listed as "Furnished apartment for quiet female student, private entrance," or "Clean apartment in private home for responsible adult." Often the owners furnish their rental units with their own unneeded belongings. For single women especially, apartments such as these offer comfortable, economical housing in a secure and respectable neighborhood.

What's new about accessory apartments is little more than the name and their appeal to a broader spectrum of people than in the past.

Many large single-family dwellings are occupied by older people whose children have moved away, or by single parents who are left with a lot of unused rooms. They don't want to leave their homes, despite escalating energy costs and taxes. And it is often questionable whether they could sell even if they wanted to, given the current low demand for large homes. For this reason, many of these homeowners are installing accessory apartments. There are 15,000 of them on Long Island, New York, and estimates of the number nationwide are as high as 2.5 to 3 million.

I am interested in installing an accessory apartment, but won't it be expensive?

Probably not. Construction figures are quickly dated, but at this writing, it is estimated that the average cost of constructing an accessory apartment is around $16,500. Obviously the actual expense will vary substantially from house to house. In most cases, you will have to add a kitchen, costing in the neighborhood of $3,200. Frequently an existing bathroom can be incorporated in the design, but if not, putting one in would run around $2,300. Some new walls may be required, or you might just permanently seal off a connecting door. A private entrance may necessitate outside steps, a porch, or a new door.

But don't forget that you can anticipate a rental income of several hundred dollars a month from the apartment. So if you need to obtain financing for the initial construction, you can, secure in the knowledge that payments on the loan will be less than the rent you collect:

Typical cost of construction	$16,500
Cost financed at 15 percent	
for 10 years, monthly payment	$266
Payment over 12 months	$3,192
Monthly rent	$400
Payment over 12 months	$4,800

The difference between mortgage payments and rental income is about $1,600 per year. After costs for maintenance and so forth are taken out, you should have an income of at least $1,200 per year or about $100 per month, without taking into account tax savings you may have from depreciation.

Professional developers would enjoy your position. Developers typically have to spend some $40,000 to $60,000 to construct one apartment in a complex. It is a mass-produced unit, not nearly so nice as yours, and would typically be located in a less desirable neighborhood than your home. The developers often have to ask so much in rent that they find few takers. In contrast, $400 per month is a very conservative estimate of the rental income from an accessory apartment in many areas, and you should have many prospective tenants among whom to choose.

I'm convinced, but I'm an older person. What about my children? How am I going to get them to go along with this? They are pretty sentimental about the house and may object to my altering it.

They may not object as much as you fear. In the first place, they may feel as unhappy as you do about your staying in the house alone. Knowing that someone is living nearby might ease a lot of concerns they are hesitant to voice to you. Also, they are certainly aware of the housekeeping burdens and expenses the house presents for you.

Your family may not only support your decision but be willing to assist you with some aspects of it as well. Include them in your planning, and don't be afraid to ask them for help. They may well be delighted to be able to participate in decision making that would ease their concerns about your security and well-being.

My kids will be so upset if I rent out "their" rooms. Of course they no longer live here, but they are always welcome and the rooms are just as they were when they lived here.

That's a sensitive issue for many parents. The house is yours in name, but you feel you share it in spirit with your children. And in that spirit, perhaps you should sit down with them and discuss your needs and possible plans for the house. They may prefer your altering their rooms to giving up the house completely. Together, you can plan a design that alters the house as they've known it as little as possible.

I really hate to think of not having spare bedrooms for my children and grandchildren when they visit.

This too is a difficult trade-off for many homeowners. It is wonderful to have extra space available for company. But when you have visitors only a few times a year, it is not always worth the effort of keeping the room clean and heated. And while it is convenient for the whole family to stay together, it may also be a strain for all of you.

Would it make more sense for the visitors—or at least some of them—to stay in a nearby motel during their visits? The rental income would more than pay for their stay.

Right now, we need money to widen doorways to accommodate my wife's wheelchair. When that loan is paid off, maybe we will talk about remodeling the basement for an apartment.

Why not do it all with one loan? You can make one plan to create the apartment and eliminate barriers, and then have the rental income to help you pay off both loans. Also, in renting the apartment, you could look for tenants who can take on tasks you cannot perform yourself. For example, you might find tenants who will look in on your wife if you are away for a weekend. This will lighten your responsibilities and prolong your independence and hers.

My husband and I would like to buy a home with an accessory apartment, but how can we find one?

Tell a real estate agent what you are looking for, and why. Most agents can use the multiple listing service computers to search for homes that either have an accessory apartment or are designed in a way that permits one to be installed easily. Typical features to look for are second kitchens, rec rooms with wet bars and full baths, and basements with outside entrances. Most multiple listing services will also note if there is an income-producing unit.

If accessory apartments can help young homebuyers so much, why haven't I read more about them in real estate magazines?

We don't know. However, in several communities the people who administer zoning ordinances on accessory apartments have stated that they get many calls from homebuyers looking for homes with apartments already installed. The Canadian Mortgage and Housing Corporation has recently commissioned a study on building new homes designed so they can be used either with or without accessory apartments. And in many upscale urban neighborhoods, such as Georgetown in Washington, D.C., accessory apartments are extremely common.

The income from an accessory apartment might let my kids and me hang on to the house in the wake of my recent divorce. But how can I, as a single parent, raise the money to install an accessory apartment? Like many other single parents trying to raise a family alone, I can hardly make ends meet as it is.

The routes that are open to you to get financing are no better than those open to most other people, and perhaps not as good. There may be questions about your ability to repay the loan because you already have a tight budget.

The ways to get financing are described in Chapter 6. What you will have to do is make as good a case as possible to your loan officer that you will make a substantial income off the apartment. Besides, the tighter your budget, the more careful a job of researching the apartment you should do, to insure that it will give you the benefits you want. If you can install an apartment inexpensively, and are in a neighborhood where you can charge a high rent, you can make a convincing case. That case can be used with a sympathetic lender, who may not necessarily be a bank. Even if your presentation does not convince a bank, you may be able to convince a friend or relative.

You also have another alternative. You can think about taking in a roomer for long enough to raise some or all of the money to install the apartment. You will have to give up some privacy, but you may be able to define the roomer's space, and you can provide the roomer with things such as a hot plate and a small refrigerator so that you minimize his or her interference with your family life. Once you have saved up enough to install the apartment, you can rescue your privacy, and have some extra income.

I am a single parent with two kids under 12. How will my kids feel about having part of the house taken for an accessory apartment, and having strange people in places that used to be their home?

You can probably answer this question better than anyone. But there is another question you should ask yourself, and also perhaps discuss with your kids: What are your choices? Are you and your kids in a position where you might have to move, and therefore leave many of your friends and theirs? Would giving up some space in the house be a better choice? Similarly, even if there is no question of moving, would the added income be worth more to you than the lost space?

My husband died recently, and my mother is getting on in years. I have a daughter who still lives with me and a son who often comes back from college. I'd like to buy a house with an apartment for my mother, but I can't find any I like. Would a bank give me financing for installing the apartment as part of the mortgage I use to purchase a new house?

You could probably find a bank that would do this, but the search would be a long one, and it might not be worth the trouble. The best thing to do in most cases is to buy a house that you can convert inexpensively, and make the renovations once you own the home.

Chapter 6, on costs and financing, will give you some idea of what it would cost to convert a home you like. However, you should probably get firm bids from a contractor, as explained in Chapter 8, "Finding a Contractor," before you go ahead and make the purchase.

It would be easy to separate off a portion of my house for a small apartment, but that would still leave me with a lot more space than I need. Could I move into the smaller apartment and rent the rest of the house—furnished or unfurnished—to a family?

That makes a lot of sense for many people. It probably will not be difficult for you to get a good income from the larger space. Many families can't afford the down payment for a house of their own. Few apartments contain more than two bedrooms, and families with two or more children are often hard-pressed to find suitable housing. The same goes for people who need space for entertaining or who enjoy gardening and yard work.

Even if you prefer for now to remain in the larger part of your house, you can certainly keep open the option of moving into the smaller unit later. The point to bear in mind is that you have a good bit of flexibility in choosing *how* you will live without altering *where* you live. As you think about alternatives in developing your house, consider each living space as a possible home for yourself and whether it would fit your needs, both now and in the future.

The couple down the street have an apartment in their basement. The last people they rented it to had people coming and going all the time and left the place a shambles. Do I need all that trouble?

No, you don't, but it's preventable. Of course you want to be choosy about who shares your house. Unlike commercial landlords, you can legally refuse to rent to people you don't feel good about, and you can put conditions in the lease to fit your circumstances and preferences. If you need help in finding the right tenant, a "matchmaking" service may be available in your community.

Before you seek tenants, sit down and make a list of things that would disturb you. Really think it through. Don't hesitate to include things which seem picky or trivial. Remember, this is your house; you will be living in it in close proximity with other people. There's no sense in letting nagging irritations spoil the arrangement, and it will just strain the relationship if you start adding "don'ts" after the tenants move in.

So incorporate all of your wishes in the rental contract itself. If you can sleep through anything but wish reasonable quiet in the house during the early evening, put that condition in. You can forbid decor changes without your express permission. You can restrict playing in the backyard to avoid damage to your prize roses. You can prohibit smoking.

Then, when you get likely prospects for the apartment, get to know them before committing yourself. If there will be more than one tenant, insist on spending some time with each of them or with the entire family. Ask for references from previous landlords. And be sure to get a security deposit. The usual practice is to require one month's rent in addition to the rent itself, which is due in advance. The deposit should repair damage in excess of ordinary wear and tear after the tenant moves out. Return the unused money, plus any interest, to the tenant.

My children have grown and moved away. I miss having kids in the house and would love to have a nice family living here. But children can be rowdy. I wouldn't have any control over them, and they might tear up the house or disturb the neighbors.

A lot of people share your concerns. The result is that many apartment complexes and private landlords will not accept families with children. But here you have an advantage over commercial renters. You can be selective about your tenants and have more control over their behavior.

Give some thought to what age children would fit in with your lifestyle. If, in fact, you like children, you might offer to baby-sit periodically. But again, put the terms of your agreement in writing and make them clear and firm. If you will not allow children, put that in the agreement. If you will, and will baby-sit, how often and for how long will you keep the children? Be specific in writing about the limits of your commitment. More than one "neighborly" relationship has fallen victim to the natural desire of a harried parent to forget that "keeping an eye on the kids" is a service and a responsibility which should be recognized and compensated as such. Regardless of kids, the key to any successful relationship is making the initial effort to be sure expectations are clear, compatible, and well-defined.

How can I be sure that my tenants will keep their part of the agreement?

Get it in writing! This is the first rule of any business relationship. Any condition that is important to you should be contained in the lease agreement. Who is responsible for repairs? Is the tenant agreeing to take you to the doctor twice a week? To buy groceries? To mow the lawn? Are you offering to baby-sit up to four hours per week—but no more? Do you want the house quiet after 10 p.m.? All cars in the garage? No playing on the lawn?

Anything which is legally included in the lease can be enforced, and violations of the agreement by the tenant can be grounds for eviction. Have your agreement checked out by a lawyer. Make it clear to the tenants that you will hold them strictly to the agreement. And do it. If you mutually agree to change the terms of the lease, draw up a new document with the changes spelled out. Don't just let things slide until the relationship becomes unbearable.

What do I need to consider in determining whether an accessory apartment would be good for me?

The *first* step is for you to decide what you would want out of the accessory apartment and what is practically feasible. What section(s) of the house would lend themselves to being separated as an independent dwelling? You will need to arrange, at the minimum, for a private entrance, a living room and/or bedroom, a kitchen, a bathroom, and closets. Check the newspapers or telephone a couple of real estate agents who manage rentals, and find out what you could charge for your unit, given its size and location and the general availability of housing.

To whom would you consider renting? Do you prefer a single person, student, family, single parent with a child, older couple? Does the apartment as you see it meet the needs of such a household? Are you near schools, businesses, colleges?

What do you want out of the arrangement? If you would like companionship, a studio apartment geared toward student occupancy may not be your best route. Do you want to appeal to a "luxury apartment" market? While you are talking to real estate agents, get a feel for what basic housing needs exist in your area. Try to work toward a layout which will be as flexible as possible.

Your second step should be to check into local zoning ordinances. You may have to meet certain conditions in order to comply with them.

Many local ordinances prohibit rental units in single-family homes, although this has not kept many homeowners from quietly renting. If accessory apartments are illegal in your neighborhood, don't give up on the idea: You can either apply for a variance or, after considering the penalty, risk installing an apartment illegally.

You mentioned that accessory apartments are illegal in many neighborhoods. How can I get information about their status in my community?

You can probably call your local zoning board or city hall and ask if it is legal to have an apartment within a single-family home in your neighborhood. If the neighborhood is zoned for single-family homes, chances are that accessory apartments are not legal. But if they are, the zoning office can tell you what conditions you must meet in order to comply with them.

If they are not legal, you have two choices. First, you can apply to the zoning board for a variance. A variance is permission to vary from zoning, typically due to hardship imposed by the land itself, such as an odd-shaped lot. But hardship is occasionally, if not properly by legal standards, interpreted in terms of the owner's circumstances. If you make a clear case that you will have to leave your long-term residence and your neighborhood unless you are granted a variance, you will have a chance of getting one. The objective of zoning is to protect neighborhoods. It will be hard to deny a variance in order to protect a neighborhood when doing so means a long-term neighborhood resident will be forced out of his or her home. You can also rely on the building national awareness of the need to permit older homeowners to have accessory apartments. They are supported by such organizations as the National Council on the Aging and the American Association of Retired Persons. In applying for a variance, it will also be worthwhile to seek your neighbors' support in advance, as well as the support of your civic association.

The alternative route is simply to install the accessory apartment illegally. We do not recommend this, as discussed later. Nonetheless, the history of most communities indicates that there is very little chance that you will be caught. The first issue here is your personal willingness to disregard zoning regulations that may be outdated. You will not be alone in doing so. Illegal accessory apartments are common in towns like Westport, Connecticut, where the head of the League of Women Voters described them as "illegal, but not very illegal."

You should also assess what will happen if your illegal apartment is discovered. First, check on the penalties for zoning violations. Chances are that the authorities will simply require you to stop renting the unit. Your loss will be what you have invested in creating the apartment minus what you have already gotten back in rent and services. If the apartment does not cost much to install, you will recover your investment rapidly and, therefore, your risks are low.

For example, if an apartment costs $2,400 to install and rents for $300 per month, in eight months you will have paid off your initial investment. If you believe, as perhaps a million American homeowners apparently do, that you are unlikely to be caught, then it is worth your while to take the risk of installing an accessory apartment. This is particularly true since many communities are changing their zoning to make accessory apartments legal.

There is also one other risk you should assess, and that is the chance that your insurance may be voided by having an illegal apartment. You should check your policy, and perhaps talk to your agent.

If it seems feasible, what should I do next?

Once you have some idea of what you want to do, it is time to have an architect or builder visit your house and estimate the cost of the necessary alterations. Of course, if you intend to install the apartment yourself, this may not be necessary. Assuming you do need help, tell the architect or builder your plans, the type of occupant(s) you wish to attract, the portion(s) of your house you feel most comfortable about renting out, and any other conditions relevant to the size, location, and room arrangement of the apartment.

An architect or builder can also assess the problems you may face in bringing the unit into compliance with local housing and fire codes. He or she can evaluate the adequacy of the current electrical and sewer systems and tell you whether major alterations will be necessary. While you are at it, you might discuss the feasibility of installing accessories which would make the unit barrier-free for a handicapped person.

Armed with the architect's or builder's estimate, you can approach lending institutions about financing. Your own bank would be the most likely starting point. A savings and loan institution or credit union which you have patronized would be a similarly logical choice. Tell the officer you want a home improvement loan. Take in a written and signed estimate from the architect, a detailed drawing of the proposed renovations, and a description of your plans for renting the apartment. The lender will be concerned with whether your apartment will in fact be marketable and whether the rent you take in will easily cover the payments on the loan. Any information you can give about the local housing market will help your case.

Then, assuming you get the loan, your next step will be to select a general contractor to oversee the construction. The contractor, in turn, will subcontract out certain aspects of the work, such as electrical engineering, plumbing, and installation of appliances. He or she should be someone you can trust and work with, because he or she will have control over who does the work, the quality of their labor, and their working conditions. The contractor should ensure that your house and yard remain habitable and reasonably free of unsightly debris and should be willing to guarantee the quality of workmanship.

My house is enough trouble to maintain with just me living in it. The hassle of overseeing tenants and having to fix every little thing that goes wrong sounds like just so much more trouble.

Being a landlord will be a new role for most accessory apartment owners. How much trouble it is depends heavily on the quality of tenants you select. In order to assist people in your situation, some communities now have public and/or private professional household matching agencies that link up prospective landlords and tenants in private homes. For a nominal sum, they determine the type of tenant who would be suitable for the apartment. Then they screen applicants who meet these requirements and appear to be compatible with the owner. Only then is an interview arranged. If the tenancy doesn't work out, the agency may repeat the procedure at no additional charge.

The agency may also help homeowners prepare rental agreements which reflect the individual's terms and preferences. If the homeowner is willing to provide baby-sitting services or the tenant agrees to take the homeowner to the doctor once a week, this arrangement can be included in the formal agreement.

Bear in mind that rental income will make it financially easier for you to maintain your house. To forestall trouble, ask your contractor whether it would be advisable to make other improvements in the house while the construction on the apartment is in progress.

You might minimize your repair burdens by making your tenant responsible for small repairs to the apartment. Or, if you feel bogged down by upkeep in general, you could seek out a tenant who will do basic maintenance tasks for you, including larger special projects such as painting the house.

HOW TO THINK ABOUT IT

The chapter that follows will discuss in detail the process of installing an accessory apartment and the problems and the benefits of having one. But first there are general issues that need to be discussed. This chapter will give you a chance to roll over in your mind problems that will come up again and again for many people as they go about installing an apartment and will also help you make the process of installing the apartment more enjoyable.

The Hidden Costs of Accessory Apartments

New Skills Required

The process of installing an accessory apartment will probably require you to learn new skills. You will have to be, or employ someone to be, an architect, a contractor, a financier, and a landlord. It you opt to do it yourself, you may also have to learn new building skills. You will probably have to learn a little more about the tax laws to take advantage of possible benefits. Even if you hire someone else to do these jobs for you, you will still have to see that they are done properly. Each of these areas has unlimited possibilities for sticky details that make the simple idea of installing an accessory apartment a great deal less simple.

Each of these required skills represents a challenge. How much do you want to learn about how best to get a loan to install an apartment? How much do you want to learn about the different kinds of kitchens you can install or whether or not it is worth putting in a microwave in order to attract as tenants young professionals with little time to cook? How much time do you want to spend checking newspaper ads and local apartment buildings to estimate how much rent you should charge?

The typical homeowner does not want to spend much time with these details. Looking up rents in the classifieds is never going to replace crossword puzzles as a leisure activity. Knowing that in your county a window has to be less than 44 inches off the floor to be considered a fire escape will not make a good story to tell at parties.

Is It Worth the Cost of Your Time?

What does make a good story to tell friends is how the fact that you did not know such details resulted in your having to install a permanent step or rebuild a window that was 45 inches off the floor. People pay a high price for the privilege of telling such stories! They have to live through them first.

Other parts of this book talk about costs in a variety of areas, such as construction, financing, and taxes. The one thing not discussed in much detail, except in this chapter, is the cost to you personally as a homeowner, in terms of your own time and frustration, of installing an accessory apartment.

There is a great deal to learn, and there are a great many potential problems. There are also a great many benefits at the end of the road. In particular, there will be dollars in your hand from the rent. The question is, Will the benefits justify your trouble? How do you add on to the costs of installing an apartment the costs of the time it will take you to make it happen, and the time it will take to manage the apartment once it is installed? How do you justify the time it will take to learn all the details, such as the 44-inch window height? How much rental income and security is worth all that effort? It is hard to say how each of us values his or her time, and the degree to which we want it to be protected from having to deal with local government bureaucracies and from having to collect rent from tenants.

There will also be some satisfaction in simply having installed the apartment, as there is in meeting almost any challenge. But that may not be enough. In summary, installing an accessory apartment is going to entail some costs for you as a homeowner that are not discussed anywhere else, in part because they are so difficult to estimate and so different for each individual. As you think about installing an accessory apartment, do not forget these costs to you personally.

Being Comfortable with the Idea of an Accessory Apartment

Know Yourself

You should be sure that the idea of having an accessory apartment feels comfortable before you start. Being comfortable with the idea of an accessory apartment in the long run comes down to two things for most people: first, managing the tenant; and second, giving up some privacy. Often, the two fears are related. Remember the advertisements for long-distance phone calls—"Reach out, reach out and touch someone"? They were always shown with a tearjerker scene that looked like a Norman Rockwell painting come to life. They were effective. But the "touching" was always at long distance. No TV personality was there pointing out that if the conversation doesn't go well, you can always hang up. It is not so easy to cut off communication with someone who lives on the other side of a party wall, shares your washer and dryer and parking, and pays you rent every month.

As a homeowner with an accessory apartment, you will have to structure the relationship you have with your tenant or tenants. You will have to make it work for you and for whoever rents the apartment. The tenant will play a major part, but you will be the captain of the ship. If you want privacy, you will have to be able to ask for it, and perhaps to insist on it. If the idea of doing that makes you nervous, you may never feel comfortable with an accessory apartment.

On the other hand, you might. The trick here—and it is a trick, simple and mechanical—is to remember that you want privacy, to write down literally what that means to you, and to make it part of the rental agreement. Most tenants want it too. Good fences make good neighbors.

Look at it another way. "Privacy" is a very general term. What it probably comes down to in most cases is that you don't want anyone's nose in your business, or, more specifically, noticing that your lawn isn't cut or that you broke down and screamed at your sister last week about what a brat her daughter is. Finally, you don't want anyone looking in your windows when he or she walks back to the side entrance that is the way to get to the apartment.

Some of this is easily solved. Put up shades in the window. If you have a tendency to lose your temper, stipulate in the lease that one loud argument of 15 minutes per month within each household will be tolerated by both landlord and tenant and ignored on either side, so long as it takes place before 10 p.m. Some privacy problems are more difficult to solve, however, and may require some more significant compromises on your part.

In summary, define what privacy means to you personally, and what it will mean to a tenant living in your home. If you can define it well, you will probably be a good landlord. You can work out mechanical solutions to address the issue, and incorporate them in the arrangement. One woman would only take single tenants who promised to be at work five days a week so she could have the house to herself during the day. If you make a virtue of your desire for privacy, you may also be offering something that works for tenants too.

If you can't define your need for privacy in practical ways, you may not be a good candidate for owning an accessory apartment.

The Possible Future

Households under pressure don't like to look at the future. It often involves taking action that in the short run adds to the pressure. A sailor on a small boat in a cold storm often hates to think about going up forward, on that narrow little triangle in the bow that continually dips under waves in freezing showers of spray, to lower sail and make the boat safer and its motion more comfortable. The sailor will put off thinking about it, often enduring a miserable time to avoid a short period of greater discomfort.

Similarly, one woman who ended up installing an apartment in her five-bedroom house had first spent years worrying about her lack of money. She was a single parent with two children who was used to the luxury of the space, and she preferred the frustration of trying to argue an ex-husband into additional support to losing the space. In the end, because she had a house that converted easily, she got $400 per month in extra income. She had to give up something for it, but having installed the apartment, with the money in her pocket, she had no second thoughts except the feeling that it was nice to have less housecleaning to do.

Older people are often in the same position. People become frail and need support and security. No one wants to admit it, and there is obviously a great deal of value in fighting this tendency through exercise and trips and anything else that keeps a person feeling young. However, you can feel a great deal younger if you have a couple of thousand dollars in rental income with which to take a trip than you will if you sit alone in a big house worrying about whether you will get along with a tenant. Income aside, for security in case of accidents when alone, or in case of criminal intrusion, there is a great deal to be said for having a tenant next door. There is not much to be said for postponing installation of an accessory apartment when you need the income and the assistance to maintain a single-family house you can no longer maintain yourself or afford to pay someone to maintain.

If you are a homeowner with the space for an accessory apartment, it is worth looking at what the future holds for you. If it holds problems an accessory apartment can help you with, don't put off installing one time after time. There is no denying that an apartment may have some drawbacks and that other solutions may come along. You may even win a lottery, but the chances aren't great. Getting some extra money and security from an accessory apartment has a lower payoff than winning the lottery, but the odds are much better. There is an advertisement for body-building equipment that shows a male teenager with a great body. Underneath it says, "No pain, no gain." The unstated message is that the gain is more than worth the pain. There are few investments that will give homeowners the same kind of gain for their pain.

Saving Money or Saving Time

Many homeowners are used to taking care of themselves. They are used to fixing things and the do-it-yourself creed. They are practical people who expect local government forms and officials to be equally straightforward. They see most of life as common sense, and will expect that installing an apartment will just take a little more common sense than usual.

Everything is common sense once you understand it. The ropes on a sailboat are all common sense when you pull on them one at a time and the sea is easy and there is someone along with nothing to do but explain what is happening. It is different when you have to use the sheets and the halyards together while relying on your memory of a one-time explanation.

Like ropes on a sailboat, accessory apartments can create too many little bits of common sense to learn at one time. You can end up with the agony of feeling no confidence in the decisions you are making. The alternative to taking the time to investigate each part of the process carefully is to hire someone to help you, whether it's an architect, a remodeler, a real estate manager to find and manage your tenant, or all three. This book will give you a good grounding in what you need to know, but it can't give you confidence in making specific decisions you are not used to making. In many situations, either you will have to put in a good deal of your time to feel confident or you will have to hire assistance in making decisions.

If you have more time and energy than money, it will often make sense to do more for yourself and, specifically, to do a lot of learning. If you have money but not much time, you will probably hire more assistance and do less yourself. In either case, be prepared for the choices and watch out for the frustration that is a sure sign you either have to learn more or hire more help, or both.

Getting Free Advice

Talk to People Who Know Your Needs

Your most immediate sources of help with thinking about an accessory apartment are friends and family members who know your needs. Talk to them. Every time you discuss your plans for the shape of the apartment or the amount of rent you might get, your ideas will become clearer. In consulting others, you may learn things you do not want to hear. In fact, if you are going to talk to a lot of people about the idea, you are bound to find some disagreement. Don't take any one opinion too seriously until you have heard several opinions. Then sort out in your own mind what you think is right.

In addition, don't assume that you should talk about the apartment only to people who know something about what you intend to do. Try explaining your ideas to someone who knows nothing about accessory apartments. It will give you a chance to think freely.

Talk to Professionals

Obviously, you should also talk to people who do know about remodeling and tenants and tax laws and local government regulations. How do you find these people? Some are paid to talk. Remodelers have to sell their services and you can call them up and ask them to come out. Ask two or three. Take up as little of their time as possible, but learn what you can from them in return for the opportunity they are getting to sell their services. Do the same with architects. Remember that you are offering them a chance to make money. They will be annoyed only if they feel you are exploiting your side of the deal by taking too much of their time or asking too many questions. Some may assume that you are talking only to them and that they will definitely get the job. Make it clear up front that you are only thinking about the apartment and about potential architects or contractors or real estate agents to manage the apartment. Do this when you call. Then it is their responsibility to decide how much of their time you are worth

Specific ways to find reputable contractors are discussed later. The point here is that it will help you a great deal to be able to talk to professionals, and you should not hesitate to do so as long as you make clear to them their chances of getting any compensation.

You should also feel free to call local government officials for information. Zoning and other issues are discussed in detail later, but in general, you have to talk to local government officials at some point about how your home is zoned. Some zoning officials and building inspectors may not enjoy explaining all the details of zoning regulations and building codes to someone who has no background in zoning or building. However, you are paying their salary through your taxes and you have a right to consult them.

If you call and an official sounds impatient with your questions, ask if you can call back when he or she will not be so busy. Do this when you first begin to hear frustration in the official's voice, but before he or she has made an excuse to get off. The official probably will be so surprised at finding a member of the public who is sympathetic that he or she will be happy to respond to your second call. In the interim you will have time to think over what you have already learned and to come up with new questions.

Another effective approach is to ask the official if he or she could come out and see your situation. Some local governments actually have officials whose job it is to visit homes and explain how to install an apartment that meets the code. In general, building inspectors are used to making site visits, and once you've got one at your house and away from the pressure of other work and phone calls, you can get a great deal more help.

Finding Homeowners to Talk to Who Have Accessory Apartments

The advice of another homeowner who has installed an accessory apartment can be invaluable, particularly if you talk to someone like yourself. If you are a single parent, find a single parent who has one. If you are an empty nester couple in your fifties, look for someone else in the same age group.

How do you find such people? If accessory apartments are legal in your community, the list of people who have obtained permits for apartments is public information. You can simply look up the list at the planning commission or zoning board of appeals, write down some names, and then start making phone calls.

You may not have to do even that much work, however. When you are talking to building inspectors, architects, and contractors, ask them if they know of anybody like you who has an apartment and might be willing to talk to you. You should also think about your friends and whether or not any of them have accessory apartments. Look in the newspaper for advertisements for separate apartments available in private homes. Call and ask the owner if you can come over and look at the apartment and talk. Most people are flattered to be asked for advice and to be seen as a pioneer.

Also look in the sale ads for homes with separate apartments. When you find one listed, call the agent and ask if you can see it. Explain your reasons, and also ask if he or she would give you the owner's name so you can find out how the apartment worked for the owner. In this case you don't have much to offer the agent in return, but remember that real estate agents are always eager to meet people because it may eventually lead to listings. In addition, you could let drop that you are talking to a lot of people about accessory apartments these days, and that if the house is a good one, you will get the word about it on the network of people interested in them. Many young homebuyers are looking for houses that have some rental income to help meet mortgage payments, and they are likely to be talking to the same people you are.

The reason for emphasizing so heavily the opportunity to talk to other people about installing an apartment is that the information in this book will not be very useful until you begin to work with it. You could know everything in the book and still end up uneasy making a decision because you haven't worked with the information. Talking with people about accessory apartments will be the equivalent of doing examples of math problems as a child in school. It will give you some experience in working with what you are learning.

HOW TO PLAN
THE APARTMENT

The planning stage may be the most enjoyable part of installing an accessory apartment, because it gives you a chance to be creative. You will be looking at the floor plan of your home to see how another separate housing unit can be carved out in your extra space. You may also want to think about the part of the house you will live in and whether or not you want to improve it at the same time.

Almost everybody has some sense of what they think a house or a home should look like and how it should be designed. In addition it sometimes seems that the number of books and magazines on remodeling homes far exceeds the number of homes out there to be remodeled. Magazines are generally best for design ideas. For hard technical information, one book recommended by an architect who has specialized in accessory apartments is *Home Renovation* by Francis D. K. Ching and Dale E. Miller.

Pages 26–39 illustrate how accessory apartments can be fitted into a variety of house types—some typical problems and solutions are discussed. Take plenty of time to look at them because they will help you think about the possibilities in your own home.

Accessory apartment plans are drawn
at ⅛ inch = 1 foot.

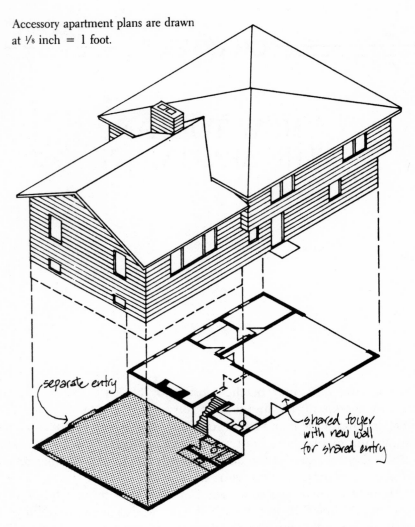

separate entry

shared foyer
with new wall
for shared entry

Split Level House.- Lower Level Conversions

    The lower levels of split level houses lend them-
selves to accessory apartments because they are easily
separated from the Main House and often already have a
bathroom or wet bar. A plan for a Rec Room conversion
is shown on the opposite page. Entry may be shared through a
common foyer, or separate, by creating a new entry for the lower level.

26

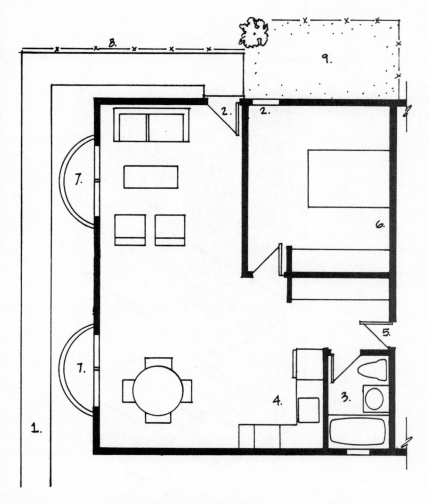

Features: Split Level / Rec Room Conversions

1. New Path to Street.
2. Rec Room Sliding Door Replaced by Single Entry Door and Window for Bedroom.
3. Existing Bathroom.
4. Wet Bar Expanded to Full Kitchen.
5. New Soundproof Door to Main House.
6. Optional new Insulation in Stud Wall to Increase Acoustical Privacy Between Units.
7. Optional Window Walls for Larger Windows in Living and Dining Areas.
8. Fence to Screen Apartment from Back Yard.
9. Outdoor Area for Apartment.

27

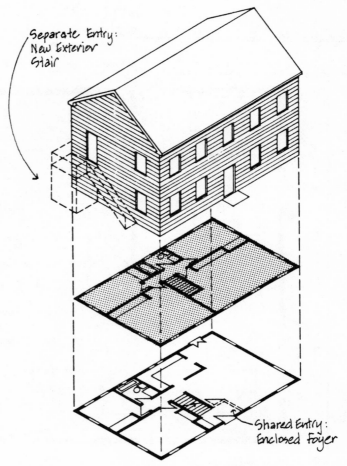

Separate Entry:
New Exterior
Stair

Shared Entry:
Enclosed Foyer

Two Story House - Second Floor Conversions

Conversion of a second floor is another approach to creating an accessory apartment. A plan for a two bedroom apartment on the second floor is shown on the opposite page. The spaciousness of an entire floor permits a variety of layouts.

Entry may be through a shared foyer at the front door with the apartment accessed by the existing stair of the Main House. Alternatively, a new exterior stair may be provided.

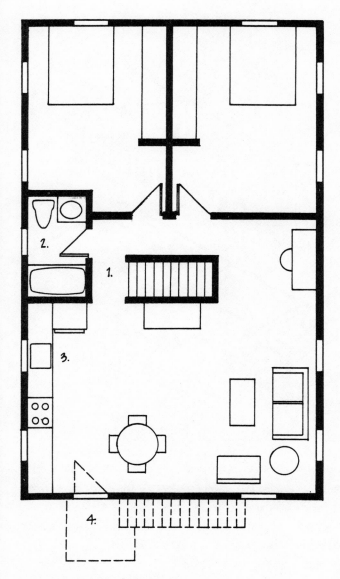

Features: Second Floor Conversions

1. Entry from Existing House Stair.
2. Existing Bathroom.
3. New Kitchen Sink near Existing Plumbing.

4. Alternate Entry Created by Construction of Exterior Stair. A new exterior stair could also be located on the back of the house.

29

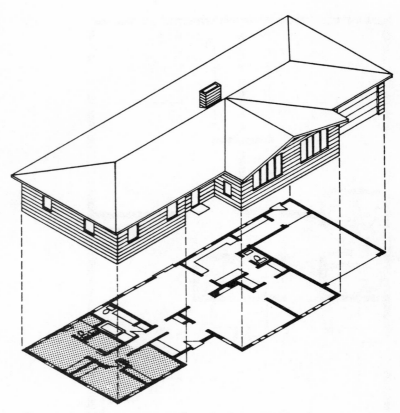

Ranch House - First Floor Conversions.

The sprawling wings of many one story houses can often be turned into accessory apartments. A plan for the conversion of the bedroom zone of this one level house is shown on the opposite page. This would require creating a new bedroom for the Main House which could be done by subdividing the Family Room. Conversion of the garage area would also be feasible.

Separate entries are easy to accomplish because both units are located at grade.

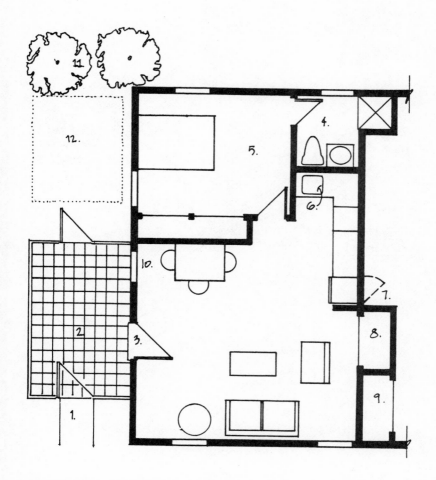

Features: First Floor Conversions

1. New Path to Street.
2. New Gate and Patio.
3. New Front Door Replaces Existing Window.
4. Existing Bathroom.
5. Bedroom Located Adjacent to Bath.
6. Kitchen Sink on Existing Plumbing Wall.
7. Soundproof Door to Main House (behind refrigerator).

8. New Closet for Acoustical Privacy Between Units.
9. Existing Coat Closet in Foyer of Main House.
10. Optional New Window at Dining Area.
11. Landscaping to Screen Apartment from Backyard.
12. Optional Gardening Area for Apartment.

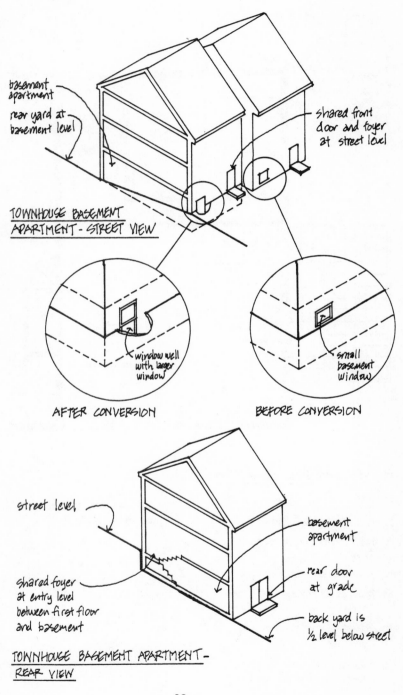

basement
apartment

rear yard at
basement level

shared front
door and foyer
at street level

TOWNHOUSE BASEMENT
APARTMENT- STREET VIEW

window well
with larger
window

small
basement
window

AFTER CONVERSION

BEFORE CONVERSION

street level

basement
apartment

rear door
at grade

shared foyer
at entry level
between first floor
and basement

back yard is
½ level below street

TOWNHOUSE BASEMENT APARTMENT-
REAR VIEW

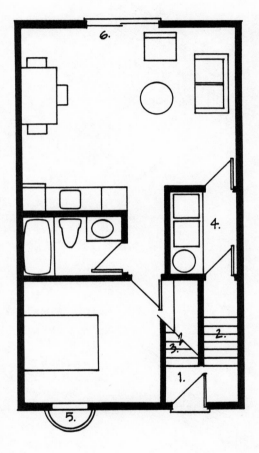

Features: Townhouse Basement Conversions

1. Shared Entry Foyer at Street Level

2. Stair Down to Basement Apartment

3. Stair Up to Main House

4. Shared Laundry

5. New Window Well for Larger Window

6. Rear Sliding Door at Grade

33

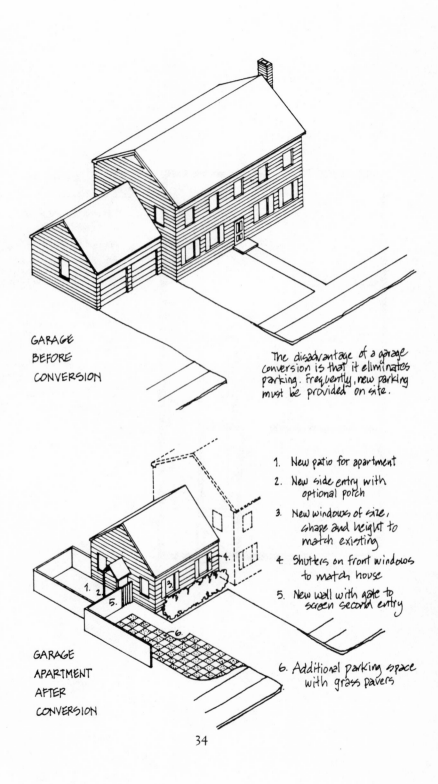

GARAGE
BEFORE
CONVERSION

The disadvantage of a garage conversion is that it eliminates parking. Frequently, new parking must be provided on site.

1. New patio for apartment

2. New side entry with optional porch

3. New windows of size, shape and height to match existing

4. Shutters on front windows to match house

5. New wall with gate to screen second entry

GARAGE
APARTMENT
AFTER
CONVERSION

6. Additional parking space with grass pavers

34

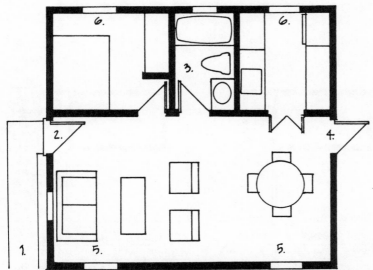

LARGE GARAGES CAN BE CONVERTED TO ONE BEDROOM APARTMENTS.

Features: Garage Conversions

1. New Path to Street.

2. New Front Door Replaces Existing Window.

3. Bath and Kitchen Located near Main House to Minimize New Plumbing.

4. Existing Door to Main House (can be retained or blocked off).

5. New Wall and Windows Replace garage Doors.

6. New Windows.

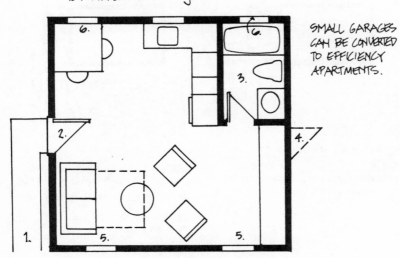

SMALL GARAGES CAN BE CONVERTED TO EFFICIENCY APARTMENTS.

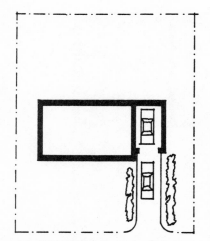

TANDEM PARKING IN EXISTING
DRIVEWAY. New landscaping and
fences can reduce the visual
impact of additional cars.

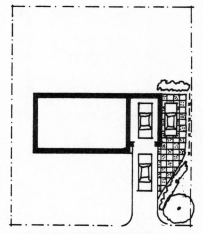

ADDITIONAL PARKING SPACE
WITHOUT WIDENING CURBCUT.
Grass pavers can be used for the
extra space. Depending on the
size of the lot, this arrangement
may still necessitate tandem
parking.

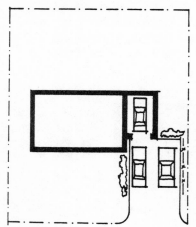

ADDITIONAL PARKING BY
WIDENING CURBCUT. This will
probably require a permit from
your local government.

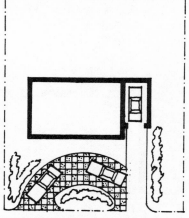

LOOP DRIVEWAY. This requires an
additional curbcut (and, most likely,
a permit). It may be difficult in
areas where parking is tight
because it reduces on-street
parking.

Landscaping Possibilities for new Parking Spaces:

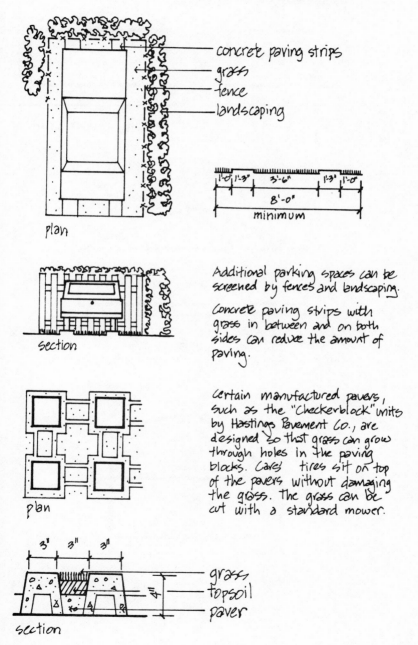

concrete paving strips
grass
fence
landscaping

8'-0"
minimum

plan

section

plan

3" 3" 3"

grass
topsoil
paver

section

Additional parking spaces can be screened by fences and landscaping.

Concrete paving strips with grass in between and on both sides can reduce the amount of paving.

Certain manufactured pavers, such as the "Checkerblock" units by Hastings Pavement Co., are designed so that grass can grow through holes in the paving blocks. Cars' tires sit on top of the pavers without damaging the grass. The grass can be cut with a standard mower.

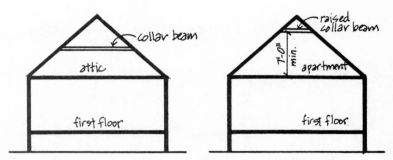

Collar beams can often be raised by using a larger beam or reinforcing other roof framing.

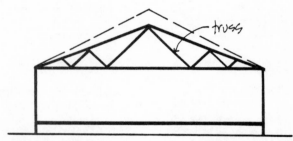

Prefabricated trusses are much more difficult and expensive to alter. Often the only approach is to remove the trusses and build a higher roof with the required headroom.

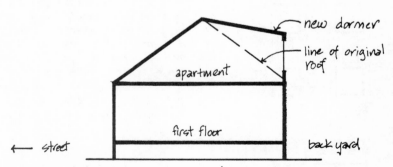

Dormers add headroom, light and ventilation to attic spaces. Various types of dormers and skylights are shown on the next page. Dormers can be added on the back side of the house so that they cannot be seen from the street.

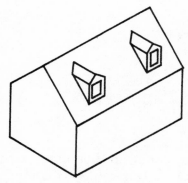

Two Small Gable Dormers

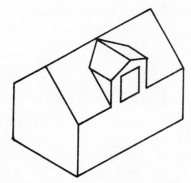

One Large Gable Dormer

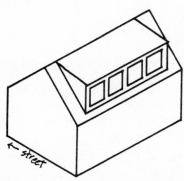

Raising the Roof from the Ridge

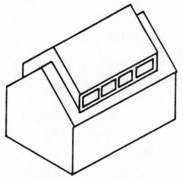

Raising the Roof Above the Ridge

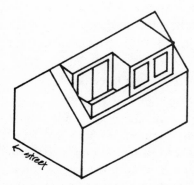

Raising the Roof from the Ridge
with an Outdoor Deck

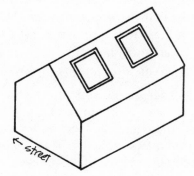

New Skylights

This chapter focuses specifically on the remodeling issues that are unique to accessory apartments. This chapter does not go into costs, which are covered in Chapter 6.

How Much Space Do You Need for Yourself?

The first question to answer in planning an apartment is how much space you need to keep for yourself. The answer to that question will determine how much space will be left for the apartment. In order to know how much space you need for yourself, you should think about how you live now and how your life may change in the future.

Meeting Current and Future Needs

The following simple questions will help you look at your house and the way you use it now:

1. Which bedrooms are used for sleeping, and which ones are used as guest rooms, storage rooms, or work rooms?

2. Do you have a basement? Is it used on a regular basis? Is it finished or unfinished? Is it dry? Does it have a bathroom, a half-bath, or a wet bar? Is the ceiling high enough for it to be used as living space? Does it have adequate windows and an outside entrance?

3. If you have a family room, do you use it often and rarely use the living room, or vice versa? Could you combine your activities in these rooms into one room to make more space available for an apartment?

4. How often is your den or study used, if you have one?

5. What space do you now use for storage, such as an attic or garage or spare bedroom, that could be remodeled into livable space? Is there another location for storing the items now in that area? Are they so valuable or so important to you emotionally that you could not give them up even if doing so meant a considerable increase in income? Are you keeping them simply because of the effort of getting rid of them, without any sense of how or when they will actually be used?

6. Could you easily add on to the side or back of your home if you had to in order to get enough space for an accessory apartment?
7. Is there a bathroom in your home that is seldom used?
8. Do you have an attic? Does it have enough headroom to be used for living space? Is it easy to get up to the attic? Is there plumbing there? Would it be possible to have a separate stair for access?
9. Do you have a garage that could be used as part of the apartment? If so, would you have enough space left over for parking without paving over much of your yard? Would parking your car outside be a problem for you? How about the other things you store in your garage, such as a lawnmower, or the papier mâché dragon from your son's sculpture class that is stuffed in the rafters over the car? Could they be stored elsewhere or disposed of?

Once you have thought about answers to these questions, think about how you might answer them five or ten years from now. How will your life-style change over the next five years, if at all? What will your life-style be in ten years? The following questions will help you anticipate possible changes in the way you will be living and therefore changes in the amount of space you might need:

1. Do you have any children living at home with you? Do you expect to have more? Will your children need more space as they grow up? Can you expect that any of them will be leaving the nest soon? Is extra income important enough to your family so that two children could make do with one bedroom?
2. How immediate is your need for income as opposed to space? If you are a single parent, is it more important for your kids to have more space in the home or more stability as a result of staying in the same neighborhood?
3. If your children have grown and left home is there a possibility of any single children moving back home with you? How about a married child or a child who is divorced? How about any other relatives? Would any of these relatives who might move in prefer to live with you or in a separate apartment?
4. Will you be retiring soon? If so, how many hours of the day will you be spending around the house? Will you be wanting more space for hobbies or for a home occupation?

5.   Will you spend most of the year at home or will you be traveling to a better climate for winters? If you are retired, will you be traveling a lot, visiting new places and visiting sons and daughters and grandchildren? Who will take care of your house?

6.   How often do you have guests overnight? How often would you like to have guests overnight? How much companionship will you get from those potential guests as opposed to someone who might live next door? How often do you expect to have guests in the future?

Accommodating Family Visitors and Other Guests

As the last series of questions indicates, there are a number of things you should take into consideration before actually designing the apartment. In some cases, a little forethought about those issues may resolve problems that might otherwise make you decide not to install an apartment.

If you are an older homeowner who has lived in the same house for years, you may find that there is a lot of sentiment tied up in some of the rooms of your home, particularly your children's rooms. Similar feelings may even be stronger in your children, for whom your house may have been the beginning of the world as they know it.

So how do you go about changing those rooms and renting them out to someone else? The first step is for both you and your children to realize that it is seldom economically feasible to allow your home to become a museum to their childhood. Emotionally it may make sense, but it is not practical when, for example, the result is a budget that is so tight that the only way you can ever visit your children is by wandering through their empty bedrooms. In fact, it may make more sense to turn those rooms into rental income that allows you to pay for visiting them.

What will you do if the rooms aren't there when family members or other guests come and you no longer have the extra bedrooms? First of all, you may find that a change in furnishings solves the problem. A sofa bed or two might be all that is needed to accommodate your guests. A second solution is to invite your guests to stay at a nearby motel. In most cases, one month's rental income would more than pay for their stay. You might even find that you are all more relaxed when you are not all in the same house.

A third solution, especially practical for holidays, is to do what one large family in Connecticut did. They arranged with the tenant as part of the lease that on Thanksgiving of every year he would go visit his own family and allow the homeowner's son and his family to use the apartment. Obviously, not every tenant will think such an arrangement is ideal. On the other hand, such a proposal might appeal to many tenants, if it meant a rent reduction during the holiday season and some extra spending money for presents. In particular, it might appeal to students, who would probably be going home for the holidays anyway and who are usually hard-pressed for money.

Using the Apartment Yourself

As you think about how much space you need, you may have the passing thought that you are well suited to live in the apartment yourself. If you are living alone, it is likely that the space in the apartment would be adequate for your needs. In this case you would be able to rent out the major portion of your home to another family and thereby bring in an even larger rental income. Many families will be looking for the opportunity your home can provide. Often families are unable to make the down payment to buy a home of their own and at the same time are unable to find an apartment with more than two bedrooms.

Even if you plan to live in the main portion of your home for now, it would be wise to consider the apartment as potential living space for yourself. If you do so, you may end up with a house that can meet both your current needs and your future ones. In one New England community, the mayor noted that many homeowners installed accessory apartments when they were in their fifties and continued living in the main part of the house. Later, in their sixties and seventies, many moved into the smaller apartment and rented out the larger part of the house. One homeowner, explaining why she was considering moving to a small apartment in part of her large house, stated that she did not want to spend her golden years cleaning three bathrooms.

In summary, if you are an empty nester or someone in your fifties or sixties, you may want to think about the apartment as a place where you yourself might want to live in the future.

The newly widowed and single parents just recovering from the financial disaster of a death or divorce may choose the opposite plan. They may want to live in the smaller apartment now as a way to hang on to the house and plan to move into the larger apartment as things improve in the future.

The same is true of a young couple wanting to use the rent from an accessory apartment to buy a house in a neighborhood they like. They may want to live in the smaller apartment at first, so they have as much extra income as possible to meet their mortgage payments. Then, as their income and family size grows, they can move into the larger apartment and eventually take over the house as a whole.

Becoming an Instant Architect

Going from general ideas about the size and location of an accessory apartment in your home to a plan requires some of the skills of an architect. For many people, they are addictive skills. It is fun to feel the power of putting lines down on paper that might control how a house or building will actually be built.

Many people already have the necessary skills. For those who don't, the basic skills aren't that difficult to learn.

What You Need to Draw Simple Plans

Three things can make it pretty easy to draw simple plans: graph paper, a mechanical pencil with a thin lead, and a good eraser. White, soft erasers are generally better than pink ones; they don't smudge as much.

Of these three tools, the only one worth spending a little extra on is the graph paper. You should look for graph paper that is tough but at the same time lets enough light through so that you can use it as tracing paper. You want the paper to be tougher than normal paper so that you can erase parts of plans again and again as you make changes, and still not have to worry about ripping the paper. You want the paper to work like tracing paper so that after getting tired of erasing you can trace the best parts of a plan onto a fresh sheet of paper. The graph paper will also help you draw straight lines, or straighter lines. If you want very straight lines, you'll need a ruler as well. The graph paper that is easiest to use will have about eight squares to the inch. Then your plans will be at the scale of one quarter inch to the foot. One inch on the paper will represent four feet in the apartment. This will be about the right size for a floor plan of the apartment and the part of your house that is next to it.

Your whole house may not fit on one page at this scale, so you may also need some tape to put a couple of sheets of paper together. Get tape with a frosted surface rather than clear tape so you can write on it. For a plan of your house and lot, showing where the parking will be, you may want to use a smaller scale, perhaps letting a sixteenth of an inch represent one foot. On the other hand, if you are doing a plan for an individual room, you may want one inch on the graph paper to represent one foot.

If you really want to get serious about playing architect, you have a couple of inexpensive choices. First, you can get a Crayola Designer Kit at a toy store. It provides a small drafting board, triangles, tracing paper, and drafting tape. Unfortunately it does not include graph paper or a scale, which is also a good thing to get if you are going to get into this seriously. However, the kit is a good, inexpensive way to have fun drafting. The kit also includes materials for drawing cars, planes, and spaceships in case you get carried away with drafting.

Another choice if you are interested in making your own plans is the Plan-A-Flex kit. It contains a marked-to-scale grid board and appropriately scaled symbols you can place on the grid for windows and doors and walls and everything else. It is available from:

The Museum Shop
The National Building Museum
Judiciary Square, NW
Washington, DC 20001

The cost is $24.95 plus $3.00 for postage and handling. For additional information, the number of the Museum Shop is (202) 272-7706.

Getting the Measurements You Need

Before you start drawing up plans, you need dimensions. You will need to know the size of the parts of your home you are going to use for the accessory apartment. You will also need the dimensions of standard fixtures and pieces of furniture. You can use a yardstick to measure the rooms, but a long tape measure will make the job go faster, particularly if you have someone working with you who can hold one end of the tape. Measuring rooms will probably take more time than you think, because you have to measure such things as where doors come in the wall and where windows are.

To get the dimensions of fixtures and furniture, you have several alternatives. You can measure the appliances, beds, chairs, and so on in your own house. Remember that these dimensions are important. You don't want to embarrass yourself in front of a contractor by proposing a bedroom that isn't big enough for a bed. Also remember that people have to be able to get around the furniture. It's no good having a bedroom with a bed in it if there is no room to get to the bed.

You can look up standard dimensions in an architectural book such as *Architectural Graphic Standards.* Architectural books are usually available in libraries, and they will generally tell both how big things are and how much space is needed around them. Finally, you can use a catalog, such as a Sears catalog, which has dimensions for everything, including the kitchen sink. In addition, such catalogs typically have dimensions for things like little refrigerators that can fit under counters and for dishwashers, cooking tops, and ovens that are combined into one space-saving unit. The Plan-A-Flex kit mentioned earlier also has scaled pieces for standard-size furniture, which you can move around.

There is a final point to remember if you have never done this kind of thing before. When you are measuring rooms and drawing them on the plan, don't forget that walls have thickness. The 6 or 8 inches a wall can take up can throw off your whole plan. Also, take the time to measure twice. If you are going to base your plans on those measurements, make sure you don't waste your time because you've made a mistake in the basic dimensions.

If you get very serious about completing all the plans for your apartment, as opposed to just doing them so you can explain your ideas to an architect or contractor, you should be sure to find out what specific drawings and plans are required by your community's ordinance when applying for zoning approval, building permits, and so forth. You need to know what drawings are required, how many of each, and at what scale.

Separate Entrances

Whether or not you are going to prepare a plan for the apartment yourself, there are some planning issues you should think about. The next few sections discuss those issues in a general way. It is important to remember, however, that the original design of your home may make many decisions on these issues for you. Most houses lend themselves to a particular means of installing an accessory apartment that is most economical. The design of the original house often makes it easy to create an apartment in one way and makes other ways of doing it much more expensive. In fact, the design of some homes makes installing any apartment too expensive to consider.

The first design issue to look at is the entrance to the apartment. This is a crucial issue, because the entrance to the apartment will affect your privacy and your tenant's, the cost of the apartment, and the exterior appearance of your house.

Your Privacy and Security Needs

A tenant living in your home will change how much privacy you have. The amount of change depends in part on how you structure your relationship with your tenant, as discussed in Chapter 10.

In addition, however, your privacy will depend a great deal on how you arrange the entranceway to the apartment. Obviously, if the tenant must cut through the living room to get to the basement stairs to the apartment, you will feel a great loss of privacy. In fact, this kind of entrance is generally not legal. If the tenant just uses your front door and then goes down the stairs to the apartment's separate door, there is little loss of privacy. If the tenant enters the home through an outside door separate from yours, there is virtually no loss of privacy.

What doors open to is an important consideration. If the tenant does go through your front door to get to the apartment, will he or she also be able to get into your living space? Will there be a front door to a small lobby with two more doors, one of which leads to your apartment, and one of which leads to the tenant's? If so, you may bump into your tenant fairly frequently, unless, as is common in many homes, you actually use the back door more often because it is nearer to where your car is parked.

A small lobby is a particularly good idea if the apartment is to be rented to a relative or someone that you expect to see a good deal. It will allow you and the person in the apartment to go into each others' homes without having to go outside if the weather is bad. In New England, many homes built in the early part of this century were designed with just such a lobby so that an apartment could be rented out to "family" or to others, if needed.

Expense of a Separate Entrance

The cost involved in creating a separate entrance varies dramatically; it depends on your floor plan. If you have a walk-out basement, you may have the entrance already. Installing a separate outside stair down to a basement will be very expensive but can also be used to get needed light into a basement.

A cheaper way to get separate access to a basement is to provide separate access from the outside to an existing interior stair. The same is true if you wish to install an apartment on the second floor. Installing new stairs is expensive.

If the stairs must be rebuilt to access an attic apartment, the cost could go above $4,000. More specific figures for entrance costs are given in Chapter 6.

Preserving the Appearance of a Single-Family Home

There is almost always someone other than the owner who is deeply concerned about how a single-family home looks. It is often the home-owner's neighbors. And it is often city hall.

Zoning ordinances that permit accessory apartments typically specify what types of changes to the exterior of your home are allowed. Generally, ordinances do not permit second front entrances facing the street or exterior stairs scaling the outside of a home. The objective is to keep the neighborhood looking just as it did. It is a clear case of "what you don't see won't hurt you."

For the same reason, other details need attention. If your garage is built into your house and you are using it for part of the accessory apartment, you will replace the garage door with a wall. If your house is brick, for example, then the wall should be brick. In addition, however, you should not leave the asphalt or concrete from the driveway leading right up to what is now a brick wall. It doesn't look right. People generally don't have driveways leading to garage doors made of brick.

As you think about the design of your apartment, remember to consider how it will look from the street. If there is anything that will give away the presence of an accessory apartment, beyond perhaps two doorbells, you will probably have problems getting it approved.

If you have to add on to your home or change any part of the exterior, there are ways to make the new parts fit in. Use the same materials in the same shades. If you have asphalt shingles on your existing roof, put asphalt shingles that are the same color, or as close as you can get, on your new roof.

If you are adding on to your home, the new roof should be of the same pitch as the rest of the roof. Overhangs—that is, the distance that the roof extends beyond the side of the house—should be the same on the addition as on the original house. New windows and doors should be of the same styles as those on the original house, particularly if they can be seen from the street.

Outdoor Space and Parking

There has been much discussion about living space in your home, but what about the use of outdoor space? It would be wise to think ahead about how you will control the use of space in your yard when you actually have a tenant. It is likely you will want to share part of the space with the tenant, particularly since this outdoor space is one reason a tenant would choose to live in an accessory apartment.

Screening for Privacy

The best way to plan for private space outdoors is to consider your own outdoor activities and then to think about what your tenant's activities might be. In particular, you might think about how providing for the latter could increase your rental incomes since outside space of one's own for gardening or sunbathing or repairing a small boat is just not available in most rental apartments.

You may feel comfortable sharing many areas, such as space for gardening, with your tenant. But other activities, such as outdoor dining, reading, or sunbathing, might be more comfortable for both parties in private space. Installation of small decks and screens may make your yard much more usable by adding to your privacy and the tenant's. And such improvements may also add to your pocketbook. The amount you can add to the rent for such "extras" will normally more than cover the cost of putting in a fence or patio.

Outdoor areas can be screened through use of fences, walls, and hedges. These three design features are well detailed in the book *Fences, Walls, and Hedges* by Jack Kramer (Scribner, 1975). Kramer describes fence designs using all kinds of materials, including wood, concrete, brick, glass, plastic, wire, and aluminum. The last four materials may surprise you, but they are often successful when combined with wood. The fences can be high or low, solid or airy. If you just need a wall that extends for a few feet to close off an entrance for your tenant, you might consider using brick, cement, decorative concrete blocks or stone.

You should also consider hedges, trees, and shrubbery. These may be more expensive initially if you have to get bushes high enough to block the view of a person standing up. You can compromise, however, by putting in a wooden fence with small, inexpensive shrubs that will grow. By the time the fence rots out, you will probably have a good hedge and won't have to replace the fence.

Tenant Parking

In some communities with accessory apartment zoning, parking for tenants' cars is not an issue. However, most communities require at least one off-street parking space for each unit, and some require one and one half parking spaces for each unit. Also, some have requirements intended to ensure that garages are not converted to accessory apartments and then front yards turned into parking lots. When you think about parking, you need to see what is required by your local ordinance. Let's assume that it requires one and one half spaces for you and one and a half for your tenant. This does not mean that the town expects you and your tenant each to own half a car. Let's also assume that you have garage parking for one car and that the zoning ordinance permits that to count for one parking space.

Is there room for two cars in your driveway? Could you arrange some sort of tandem parking in the driveway with one car parked behind another? Could you widen your driveway or pave a parking space somewhere on the lot without making it look like a shopping plaza? If you incorporated the garage in the apartment, would you be able to fit the necessary three spaces on your lot?

If you have to pave an additional space, you must consider once again whether or not you are radically altering the single-family appearance of your home. In addition, you should be sure, for your own convenience, that you are not going to plan for parking that will be a daily test of your tenant's parking skills, with you looking out the window to see whether he or she is going to scratch your car. It would probably not get zoning approval in any case.

If you do have to pave part of your yard, think about using grass pavers, or what the Hawaiians call "puka" paving: concrete paving blocks that have holes. The holes allow the grass to grow up through the blocks, while the blocks still keep the cars from turning your yard into mud. These are illustrated on page 37.

Utility Meters

When you have an accessory apartment, your utility bills will increase. Undoubtedly you will pass the increased cost on to your tenant, but what is the best way of doing that? One method is just to include the cost of utilities in the rental price. You simply average the utility bills for the year and then assign a portion of the monthly average to the tenant. Normally, the easiest way to estimate the tenant's portion is to divide the total size of your house, or its "square footage," into the size of the tenant's apartment. Then multiply the number you get by your average monthly utility bill. The result is the tenant's portion.

This is the simplest method in practical terms, but it is unlikely to be a completely accurate reflection of the cost of utilities used by the tenant. In addition, it gives the tenant no incentive to conserve energy.

The alternative is to install separate utility meters for the tenant. Then the tenant will pay for his or her own utilities. The cost of installing a separate utility meter varies. In fact, many utility companies will not even make an estimate without coming to your home. It is probable, however, that the cost will be high, perhaps as much as $500 or more. It is hard to give a decent estimate, because local costs vary enormously.

A major advantage of a separate utility meter is that you are not involved with your tenant's use of utilities. If you are the one paying the utility bills, you will be apt to worry whether the tenant will be wasteful or about whether you have charged enough for utilities in the rent.

In some localities the housing regulations, or the regulations of individual utilities, require that each housing unit have its own utility meter. Requirements for separate water meters are a particularly hard burden for homeowners who want to install an accessory apartment. Water is inexpensive enough so that it almost never justifies the cost of installing a separate meter. Yet some communities require it. In addition, some communities also require a separate sewer hookup, for which they also charge a fee, often a very high one.

In general, where separate meters are not required for electricity and gas, you should still get estimates of the cost of separate meters. Ask yourself if the cost is low enough so that it is worth spending the money to protect yourself from a tenant who may be less careful than you are about turning down the heat when it is not needed.

Regardless of your utilities, you and your tenant should have separate controls for the heat and/or air conditioning. This does not mean that you have to have separate heating systems. It simply means that if you live in Minnesota, your tenant has to have a way to turn on the heat and keep warm when you have forgotten about the furnace during your extended fall vacation in the Bahamas.

What Makes a Good Apartment?

When some apartments are advertised, hopeful tenants beat down the door. Others sit vacant for months. There are apartments where the tenants remain for ten or twenty years, while other apartments turn over two or three tenants each year. The reasons for vacancies and turnover rates vary, but one factor is always the apartment itself.

Look through some apartment advertisements in your local newspaper. Do you find certain adjectives used frequently? "Clean," "quiet," "secure," "good location," "attractive," and "sunny'" are typical ones. A fireplace is always a big attraction. Now ask yourself who would want to live in the apartment that you have in mind. Would you? What inviting features can your apartment offer to a tenant?

First, there are some features that you cannot change. One is location. In fact, you may be installing the apartment to avoid moving yourself, which is probably a sign that the location is pretty good.

There are other things you can alter but not totally change. For example, if you are offering a basement apartment you will never be able to make it as sunny as a second-floor apartment, but you can excavate soil along the side of the house to form a light well for a window. You may have to do this anyway to meet building codes. Find out how much extra it would cost to create a window to give the apartment some real light. If there is a high incidence of burglary in your neighborhood, you can add special locks to the doors and windows and install extra lighting around the entrance.

Finally, there are things over which you have complete control. These include the cleanliness of the apartment, the attractiveness of the apartment decor, to some extent the floor plan of the apartment, and the quality of the appliances and finishes.

A feature that one can often offer without much extra expense is access to a washer and dryer. In fact, a small room that includes a washer and dryer can frequently serve as a very good sound barrier between the two apartments. In this case, both apartments will need doors with locks that have access to the laundry room.

Other features you can easily offer will vary with the type of house you have and the space in which you are putting the apartment. A skylight may make an attic apartment much more attractive. One homeowner, who lived in a second-floor apartment in an attic so he could rent the downstairs for more income, got to his apartment by means of an exterior staircase in back of the house. While remodeling, he expanded the landing for the staircase into a small deck for himself. He wasn't adding something for the tenant, but the result was the same. He got more income by renting a larger space, while still having a good place to live and a deck that felt like it was in the treetops.

Basement Apartments

Many apartments are installed in basements. That is because it is often the easiest space to convert to an apartment. Look at all the advantages: It is a separate floor, it often has a separate entrance, and it easily connects to plumbing, electric, and heating lines currently used in the house. The last advantage might be "and it is hardly ever used by us!" If that thought went through your mind, you had better think about why you do not use that space yourself. Is it that you do not need the space, or is it that the space is not desirable?

The number one problem with basements is dampness. The dampness in the basement may be caused by outside moisture if your basement was not properly drained and sealed on the outside when it was built. To be properly sealed, it should have been built with drain tile around the perimeter to carry water away from the house and foundation. Additionally, the basement walls should have been waterproofed with tar and felt. Dampness is also caused by indoor uses such as washers and dryers or leaking pipes.

Another problem with basement living is lack of light and ventilation due to small windows or no windows. Out of consideration for the good health of your tenants, the building inspector will force you to add window space if it is now inadequate in your basement.

A guide to all of the regulations affecting accessory apartments for Montgomery County, Maryland, is included at the end of this chapter. The regulations in your area will almost certainly be different, but the Montgomery County guide will give you a chance to see the scope of the regulations that will affect your ability to install an apartment. It will also give you a chance to see how they are applied. Remember that the Montgomery County guide does not apply in other areas, and in any case it is subject to ongoing revision as regulations change. To get a sense of window space required and how it is defined, see item 29 of the Montgomery County guide. It requires that the minimum total window area be 8 percent of the total floor area of any room except a bathroom or kitchen.

The most straightforward way to add light to a basement is to increase the size of the window wells, if any exist. Obviously, if part of the basement is above the ground, you can install windows in that part without having to excavate or put in a window well. A window well is the area dug out around a basement window. It typically has a metal or plastic form to retain the soil and a drain to prevent the buildup of water.

You can also choose to excavate a large amount of soil to allow for a large window or even a floor-to-ceiling window or a sliding glass door in the basement. Retaining walls are required to hold back the earth; you may want to have them step down so they look less imposing. Finally, you can remove a good part of the basement wall and replace it with windows. You will have to support the floor joists with a header of some kind that bridges the remaining portions of the foundation. The best side of your house on which to put such a window is the south side, because then it will bring in more light in winter when the sun comes less from overhead and more from the south. An installation of this kind will be expensive but will make the apartment much more livable. One man installed sliding glass doors in this way, as well as a small excavated patio, for his aging mother, who was coming to live with him.

Another problem you might encounter in the basement is inadequate headroom. Pipes and ductwork usually run along the ceiling of the basement. Suspended ceiling tile is often used to cover them, but it also takes up headroom. A typical minimum ceiling height in a building code is 7 feet over most of the floor area. (The phrase "over most of the floor area" needs some explanation. Item 39 in the Montgomery County guide discusses minimum ceiling heights in some detail, and also how they are measured and what exceptions can be made. You will have to get the figures for your locality, but the Montgomery County guide should give you some feel for requirements such as minimum ceiling heights.)

Another way to deal with a low ceiling is to lower the floor level, but it will probably not be economical to do so unless the rest of the accessory apartment can be installed inexpensively. A third possibility, if the pipes and ducts themselves are high enough, is simply to paint the pipes so that they blend in with the ceiling.

Finally, you may need to resolve problems of access to any utilities in the basement, or to a washer and dryer that may be there. You will regularly need to get to the washer and dryer and on occasion to the furnace. Can you do this without having to pass through your tenant's space? Can you build these items into a separate closet to which you have access? Can you put them all in a laundry room? And, finally, can you insulate them against generating too much noise in the tenant's apartment?

Attic Apartments

Your attic, if it is like most attics, was not designed as living space. As a result, it is not only often happily available for an apartment, but also often unhappily difficult to convert to one. The critical issues are the headroom, the strength of the floor, the access stairwell, and the difficulty of putting in plumbing. Yet another issue is the noise of someone above you.

The headroom of your attic must meet with the normal ceiling requirement of at least 7 feet. It may be higher in your community. Again, see item 39 of the Montgomery County guide at the end of this chapter to understand how that requirement is varied in certain cases to permit better use of attic space.

If the headroom is currently inadequate because of beams joining the rafters together, you may be able to move them. This is illustrated on page 38. First, you must determine if you have a truss or collar-beam roof support system. Houses built as part of a recent development often have prefabricated trusses. Each piece of the truss typically provides support to other pieces in a manner that makes the movement or elimination of pieces to increase headroom almost impossible. Older homes were usually built with horizontal collar beams joining the rafters, and these can often be raised to increase headroom in the attic. If you are not a professional builder or engineer, you will need to get assistance in seeing whether you can alter the roof structure to get more headroom.

The strength of the floor in your attic depends on the size of the floor joists. The joists are the horizontal members running from wall to wall that support the boards of the floor. Floor joists in attics are occasionally not intended to carry significant weight, although in most cases they can. You will need to determine whether the floor can support the new load of furniture and people. Again, you may need professional assistance. If the joists are not strong enough, you will have to decide whether it is worth the cost of reinforcing or replacing the existing joists with new, heavier joists.

The next item for you to tackle is the stairway to the attic. The major question is whether or not it provides comfortable access. Problems might include stairs that are too steep, inadequate headroom, unsafe handrails, or poor location of access to the stairway from the second floor. The stairs must also serve as a safe fire exit when the distance from the attic windows to the ground is too far to jump. The building regulations of your community will have safety requirements for stairs. These will determine both how steep the stairs can be and what kinds of doglegs and landings are permitted. Existing stairs that are steep or have doglegs may not be permitted by the building inspector if you intend to use the attic as an apartment.

Another problem with attics is plumbing. It is often expensive to get the plumbing up there. To save as much money as possible, you should try to keep the toilet and the kitchen areas in the apartment directly over the wall which carries water and drainage pipes for the floor below. Then the plumber just has to extend the pipes straight up. Running them horizontally through the floors is not easy and can be expensive. However, often it will not be possible to keep the toilet and kitchen where the plumber would like to see them; the space in the attic may just not work that way.

Getting enough light and ventilation poses yet another problem. The few small windows in most attics will be inadequate for a room that has become living space. One popular option is to add dormer windows. These can be expensive on older houses if they are built to fit in with the original design. One way to avoid this cost is to install them facing the rear of the house so that no change is noticeable from the street and the design does not have to conform to the original style of the house. In addition, they can then be big enough to really let in some light. Dormer windows can also increase the amount of attic floor space that has adequate headroom.

Skylights are an increasingly popular way of adding light to attic areas. The skylights should be ones that open if you also expect to use them for ventilation. Many do not open. The quality of the skylight itself and the installation are critical due to the exposure it will receive as part of the roof. You would not want to have to help your tenant put buckets under a leaky skylight in the middle of a rainy night. The November 1983 issue of *Professional Remodeling* (published by Harcourt Brace & Jovanovich) has an excellent article, complete with diagrams, entitled "Light, Cool, Airy Attics Add Space and Profits." Some of the above ideas and those that follow on heating and cooling an attic are drawn from that article.

Insulation is also a critical factor in making an attic successful living space. Most older homes have inadequate insulation by today's standards. The amount of insulation you need will differ according to the specific features of your attic and the climate in which you live, but the general rule is to maximize the amount of insulation. As you are insulating, make sure that ventilation space is maintained between the insulation and the plywood sheathing or planking that covers your roof rafters. Insulation in many ways seems a simpler problem than it is. If not installed properly it can cause condensation and rot. Be sure to consult a professional if you intend to do it yourself and are not absolutely sure how to do it. What the insulation will accomplish is a more stable temperature for the attic. Cold weather is not so much of a problem for an attic as hot weather, since hot air rises to the top of your house. In the winter that's fine. But in the summer the same thing happens; in addition, the sun is shining directly onto the roof and its heat is radiating through. An extension of the central air conditioning, a window-unit air conditioner, or a ceiling fan are choices for cooling an attic in summer. Often two fans, one at either end of the attic, work well.

In order to make a successful attic apartment, you must resolve any of these problems that exist. Attics often just aren't worth the cost of converting. However, the ones that are, when they are converted with some imagination, make good, interesting apartments.

As an aside, it should be noted that often apartments that cannot be justified on the grounds of rental income are still installed for relatives. Later they end up being rented. Similarly, apartments installed for rental income often end up being used by relatives. If you are installing an apartment in an attic for a relative, and it costs more than you expect, remember that it may someday be a source of income. Likewise, an apartment you are installing for rental income is worth installing properly since it is not unlikely that it will one day be used by you or a member of your family.

Garage Apartments

Garages are not designed as living space, but they can often be successfully converted to accessory apartments. The chief advantage of a garage is that it already has a separate entrance from the outside, or at least one can easily be installed. It is usually separate from the main house and may even be detached. A garage can make a nice, clean conversion, but it often requires the added cost of restructuring the floor, the ceiling, and the walls. Tom Philbin and Fritz Koebel provide many of the suggestions given below in their article "The Convertible Garage," found in the November 1981 issue of *The Family Handyman*.

The garage floor is generally located a few steps down from the main floor of the house. If it is combined with a part of the main house, and if you live in a mild climate, you may have the option of laying tile, floor covering, or carpet directly on the concrete. In other climates you should plan to lay wooden floor joists and a wooden floor, or else the cold floor will encourage arthritis in your tenants and perhaps apoplexy in your building inspector.

Garage roofs are often pitched. You can choose to maintain this line for the interior ceiling or drop the ceiling to the conventional height of 8 feet. Once again, insulation is critical since the garage roof is exposed to direct sunlight. Finally, the interior walls need to be modified. The walls that make up the garage will need insulation and wallboard. Then you might also insert a few new interior walls to divide living spaces. A generous two-car garage may be large enough to become a small efficiency apartment by itself. Otherwise you may need to use some additional space from the main house, or else add on to the garage itself.

Properly finishing the garage floor, roof, and walls will mean heating and cooling savings in the long run. Garages were built to protect cars, not people, from the weather. When your garage becomes a living space, it must be sealed off from outside air.

As noted earlier, it is important to treat the former garage entrance properly so that it doesn't look strange from the outside. If you make the exterior look as though there had never been a garage door there, don't leave a driveway up to the new wall where the door was. If you need the driveway for parking, at least landscape the last few feet of it. If you leave the garage door and just seal it and frame in a new wall behind it, then leave the driveway as well.

Making Other Improvements While You Install the Apartment

If your house will already be opened up to a remodeler, with the accompanying disruption of normal home life, why not tackle some other projects your home has been in need of for some time?

The convenience is undeniable. Unfortunately, the added cost is equally undeniable. You may find it economical to take out a loan that will cover the apartment and the other repairs. But if the loan for the apartment is already making you nervous, avoid overextending yourself.

At a minimum, it is worthwhile looking at the things you might like to do to the house, regardless of the apartment, and estimating or getting estimates for the costs of doing them. This is particularly true for those things that will save you money, such as installing better insulation or a more efficient heating system. Once you have the estimates in hand, you can decide either to go ahead with the extras or to wait until the income from the apartment has improved your financial picture. You should also note that, in some communities, making a substantial investment in your house may trigger requirements that part or all of it be brought up to current codes.

Interior Design

Making the interior of the apartment consistent with the decoration in the rest of the house can be an advantage if it ever becomes part of the main house again. Having somewhat similar interiors can also promote a feeling of contentment on your tenant's part. Remember, unless you are intending to use the apartment to get out of a really bad financial problem, you don't want to end up living in a scruffy apartment next to a tenant who has a well-finished home.

One other note on the interior design of the apartment: Since you are making a complete living space in what is normally a small floor area, you should take size into account in decorating the apartment. A house-sized kitchen may be inappropriate for the apartment. If you are furnishing the apartment, scaled-down, functional furniture is appropriate to rooms that accommodate two or more uses, such as a living/dining room. Colors and textures should increase the perception of spaciousness; dark colors can visually rob the space. Almost any magazine on homes and home decoration can help you with this kind of design problem, especially ones such as *Apartment Living*. Here are some common suggestions:

Living room/bedrooms created with sofa beds.

Dining/study rooms created with bookshelves and a flexible table.

Light and/or monotone color schemes.

Fewer walls and partitions that cut up space.

Walls covered with mirrors.

Furniture with simple lines and/or made of see-through materials.

Barrier-Free Apartments

The saying goes that the only things that are certain are death and taxes. Recently people have remarked that since our medical research institutes have been so successful at snatching people from the jaws of death, maybe we should put them to work to find a cure for taxes. The fact is that people are living longer. According to a report of the House of Representatives Select Committee on Aging, in 1978, a 75-year-old woman had a life expectancy of another 11.5 years. In addition, over the period 1970 to 1978, the life expectancy of a woman of 75 had increased by 57.5 percent. The life expectancy of older people is increasing. As a result, we have an enormous growth in the frail elderly, as noted earlier.

The significance of that increase, if you are an older homeowner, is a growing likelihood that before you die there will be a time when you or your spouse will need a home that is designed to minimize the problems of getting up a flight of stairs, opening a cupboard, or getting in and out of the bathtub. If, for you, standing unsupported is effortless, you will not realize how difficult it is to monitor the pot that is cooking on the back burner from a wheelchair. Imagine that you are dependent on crutches, a walker, or a wheelchair to get around. Or imagine that you are just less sure on your feet. Now run through some of your daily activities at home. What physical features of your home would be barriers to normal living if you were disabled in any way?

If you are old, or even just an empty nester, think about what life will be for you. The challenge is not, as many seem to think, a question of whether as we age we are going to go out awash in a publicly supported sea of dignity, respect, and medicines. It is whether we are going to seize the opportunity of a longer life and make it worth living in our own terms.

To be specific, if you are old and hope to grow older, you should think about how to take advantage of the opportunity that installing an accessory apartment gives you to create a home in which you can enjoy growing old. It will be a great deal easier to create a barrier-free accessory apartment now than at some time in the future when you have less energy, less patience for the foibles of contractors and building inspectors, and less tolerance for living in a house that is also a remodeling project.

If, at some time in the future, you must use a wheelchair or even just a walker, stairs, narrow doorways, sills, high countertops, sinks, and cupboards may become major barriers to normal living. If you are arthritic, even doorknobs and cupboard handles can be annoyances. The following list will help you take inventory of potential barriers in the apartment or the part of the house you are keeping for yourself. Think about the value to you of creating a home, either the apartment or the part of the house you will stay in, that is barrier-free, so that you can age easily in your own home.

Below is a list of barriers and methods for removing them. These suggestions come from two sources, which are recommended reading. One is a booklet called *Designs for Independent Living* that is produced by the Whirlpool Corporation. The other is an article, "Remodelers Can Create Barrier-Free Kitchens" by Joy Schrage, in the November 1983 issue of *Professional Remodeling* (published by Harcourt Brace Jovanovich). There are also a great many other good sources on this subject available in most libraries.

Problem	*Solution*
Entrance	
Steps	Ramp
Stairs	Apartment on one floor
Doorsills	Remove, smooth over
Narrow doorways	Widen doorways (to 32 in.)
Kitchen	
Countertop too high	Lower at least one countertop (to 30 in.)
Sink or stove inaccessible by wheelchair	Remove lower cabinets, allowing wheelchair to slide underneath (pipes and heating elements must be insulated); install a mirror over the range; install a microwave oven
Floor area too narrow for wheelchair's turning radius	Widen floor space (wheelchairs work best in L- or U-shaped kitchens)
Cabinets inaccessible or difficult to open	Enlarge handles on cabinets; remove cabinet doors; make pullout cabinets; use lazy Susans
Bathroom	
Sharp edges	Modify countertop edges
Bathtubs, showers	Install grab bars; provide bathing seats and use nonslip surface in bathtub; recess soap dishes; install hand sprayer; put shower head at breast height
Toilet	Raise height (to 17–20 in.); install grab bars

One important consideration is how a disabled person or someone with limited mobility will get out of the apartment or call for help in the event of an emergency. An accessible entrance/exit is critical. A smoke detector is also essential, if it is not already required by local building regulations. Another good idea, yet more elaborate, is to install an alarm system that the disabled person can activate easily to notify the person in the adjacent unit in an emergency situation. Such an alarm is particularly appropriate for the bathroom, as accidents are very likely to happen there due to fainting, stumbling at night, and slipping on wet surfaces.

Making your apartment barrier-free will increase the installation cost, but if you are putting in a new kitchen, for example, the April 1985 issue of *Builder* magazine quotes an extra cost of only 10 percent.

If you do decide to make a barrier-free apartment, you must decide how barrier-free you want to make it. If you are thinking of it as an insurance policy for your own future, make the modifications more flexible and limited. At least make doorways wide enough and put in such features as door handles that are easy to turn even for someone with arthritis—since it won't cost you any more. If you want to go further, to justify the cost now you should probably consider whether or not you want to rent to someone who is disabled and willing to pay for the advantages and extra cost of a barrier-free apartment. At a minimum, if you are an elderly homeowner, make sure that one of the two units you will have in your house will be a practical place for a frail elderly person to live.

A Sample of Accessory Apartment Regulations

We have included this list of regulations as a guide for homeowners so they will have a sense of the kinds of regulations they are likely to have to meet to install an accessory apartment. It is a long list, but you would do most of the things specified even if no government agency required them.

It should be emphasized that these regulations apply in Montgomery County only, as of August 1985. It is a particularly useful compilation of requirements derived from several different sets of laws and regulations in the county, all of which apply to accessory apartments. Regulations in other localities will almost certainly be different. This compilation should be taken not as a guide to what is legal in other localities, but simply as a list of issues that homeowners will probably have to address. Your local government may have compiled a similar list. If so, it will be available from the agency that administers the accessory apartment ordinance.

A Guide to Use and Occupancy Certificate Inspections for Accessory Apartments Authorized by Zoning Special Exceptions in Montgomery County, Maryland

1984

Prepared by   Department of Housing & Community Development
              Department of Environmental Protection
              Department of Fire & Rescue Services

Occupancy Inspection Guidelines
for Accessory Apartments

Items apply to (Apartment or) that portion of building containing the apartment and are based on the Building, Electrical, Fire Prevention, Housing and Zoning Laws of Montgomery County, Maryland.

_____ 1. Only one accessory apartment may be created on the same lot as an existing one-family detached dwelling.

_____ 2. The accessory apartment must be internal to the main dwelling on property smaller than one acre.

_____ 3. An addition to an existing one-family detached dwelling or conversion of a separate accessory structure that existed on the lot with the main dwelling before December 2, 1983, can only be accomplished if the property is larger than one acre.

_____ 4. The existing single-family dwelling must be at least 5 years old.

_____ 5. Any separate entrance must be away from the front street.

_____ 6. All modifications must be compatible with the existing dwelling and surrounding properties.

_____ 7. The accessory apartment must have the same street address as the main house.

_____ 8. The minimum lot size is at least 7500 square feet or the minimum lot size of the zone, whichever is larger. All other development standards of setbacks, lot width, lot coverage, building height and the standards for an accessory building apply in the case of conversion of such a building.

_____ 9. There shall be no excessive concentration of accessory apartments (existing and/or approved) in the general neighborhood.

_____ 10. There must be at least two off-street parking spaces unless more spaces are required due to family use or adequate on-street parking permits fewer off-street spaces. Off-street parking is allowed in a driveway but not in a front yard.

_____ 11. The accessory apartment shall not be detrimental to the use and peaceful enjoyment of surrounding properties or the general neighborhood and shall cause no objectionable noise, traffic or other adverse impact.

_____ 12. The owner must occupy one of the dwelling units.

_____ 13. The owner must have owned the property for one year except for pre-existing apartments.

_____ 14. The owner shall receive no compensation for more than one unit.

_____ 15. Subdivision covenants: Any covenants on the lot or sub-division must be examined for restrictions or prohibitions against the proposed accessory apartment.

_____ 16. Structural members: All supporting structural members of all structures shall be kept structurally sound, free of de-terioration and maintained capable of safely bearing the dead and live loads imposed upon them.

_____ 17. Exterior surfaces (foundations, walls and roof): Every foun-dation, exterior wall, roof and all other exterior surfaces shall be maintained in a workmanlike state of maintenance and repair and shall be kept in such condition as to exclude rodents.

_____ 18. Foundation walls: All foundation walls shall be maintained so as to carry the safe design and operating dead and live loads and shall be maintained plumb and free from open cracks and breaks, so as not to be detrimental to public safety and welfare.

_____ 19. Exterior walls: Every exterior wall shall be free of holes, breaks, loose or rotting boards or timbers, and any other conditions which might admit rain or dampness to the in-terior portions of the walls or to the occupied spaces of the building. All exterior surface material, including wood, com-position, or metal siding, shall be maintained weather-proof and shall be properly surface-coated when required to pre-vent deterioration.

_____ 20. Roofs: The roof shall be structurally sound and tight and shall not have defects which might admit rain, and roof drainage shall be adequate to prevent rain water from caus-ing dampness in the walls or interior portion of the building.

_____ 21. Decorative features: All cornices, entablatures, belt courses, corbels, terra-cotta trim, wall facings and similar decorative features shall be maintained in good repair with proper an-chorage and in a safe condition.

_____ 22. Chimneys: All chimneys, cooling towers, smokestacks, and similar appurtenances shall be maintained structurally safe, sound, and in good repair; all exposed surfaces of metal or wood shall be protected from the elements and against decay or rust by periodic application of weather-coating material such as paint or similar surface treatment.

_____ 23. Stairs and porches: Every stair, porch, balcony, and all appurtenances attached thereto shall be so constructed as to be safe to use and capable of supporting the loads to which it is subjected and shall be kept in sound condition and good repair.

_____ 24. Weathertight: Every window and exterior door shall be fitted reasonably in its frame and be weathertight and weather stripping shall be used to exclude wind or rain from entering the dwelling or structure and they shall be kept in sound condition and good repair.

_____ 25. Door hardware: Every exterior door, door hinge, and door latch shall be maintained in good condition with
> ____ Front door deadbolt, vertical deadbolt, or 1″ horizontal deadbolt.
> ____ Window pins, locks, or charlie bar.
> ____ Rear-door deadbolt, vertical deadbolt, or 1″ horizontal deadbolt.
> ____ Sliding glass door pins, lock, or charlie bar.

_____ 26. Bathroom and kitchen floors: Every toilet, bathroom and kitchen floor surface shall be constructed and maintained so as to be substantially impervious to water and so as to permit such floor to be easily kept in a clean and sanitary condition.

_____ 27. Exit facilities: All interior stairs and railings and other exit facilities of every structure shall be maintained in sound condition and good repair by replacing treads and risers that evidence excessive wear or are broken, warped or loose. Every inside stair shall be so constructed and maintained as to be safe to use and capable of supporting the anticipated loads. Basement stairwells must be at least 22″ wide if used for an exit path. No furnace may be located under an exit stair.

_____ 28. Handrails/Guardrails: Handrails having minimum and maximum heights of 30 inches and 34 inches, respectively,

68

measured vertically from the nosing of the treads, shall be provided on at least one side of stairways of three or more risers. Open sides of stairs shall be protected.

Porches, balconies, or raised floor surfaces located more than 30 inches above the floor or grade below shall have guardrails not less then 42 inches in height.

Handrails and guardrails on open sides of stairways shall have intermediate rails or ornamental closures which will not allow passage of an object 9 or more inches in diameter.

_____ 29. Habitable rooms: Every habitable room shall have at least one (1) window of approved size facing directly to the outdoors or to a court. The minimum total window area, measured between stops, for every habitable room shall be eight percent (8%) of the floor area of such room, except in kitchens when artificial light may be provided. Whenever walls or other portions of a structure face a window of any room and such obstructions are located less than three (3) feet from the window and extend to a level above that of the ceiling of the room, such a window shall not be deemed to face directly to the outdoors or to a court and shall not be included as contributing to the required minimum total window area for the room.

_____ 30. Common halls and stairways: Interior common halls and stairways shall be adequately lighted at all times with an illumination of at least a sixty (60) watt light bulb. Such illumination shall be provided throughout the normally traveled stairs and passageways.

_____ 31. Habitable rooms: Every habitable room shall have at least one (1) window which can be easily opened or such other device as will adequately ventilate the room. The total openable window area in every room shall be equal to at least forty-five percent (45%) of the minimum window area size required in Number 30.

_____ 32. Screens: All openable windows and doors must be screened.

_____ 33. Window bars: Required escape windows shall not be barred except with breakaway bar systems approved by the Fire Marshal.

_____ 34. Toilet rooms: Every bathroom and water-closet compartment shall comply with the light and ventilation requirements for habitable rooms as required by Numbers 30 & 32 except that a window shall not be required in bathrooms or water-closet compartments equipped with an approved mechanical ventilation system.

_____ 35. Separation of units: Dwelling units shall be separate and apart from each other except that a common, recirculating heating, ventilation, and air conditioning system is acceptable. Units may be connected by a lockable standard interior door. Sleeping rooms shall not be used as the only means of access to other sleeping rooms or habitable spaces.

_____ 36. Basement rooms: Basement rooms partially below grade shall not be used for apartments unless
　　　1. Floors and walls are watertight so as to prevent entry of moisture.
　　　2. Required minimum window area of every habitable room is entirely above the grade of the ground adjoining such window area.

_____ 37. Area for sleeping purposes: Every room occupied for sleeping purposes by one (1) occupant shall contain at least seventy (70) square feet of floor area, and every room occupied for sleeping purposes by more than one (1) person shall contain at least fifty (50) square feet of floor area for each occupant thereof.

_____ 38. Every sleeping room and living room shall have at least one operable outside window or exterior door approved for emergency egress or rescue in accordance with the standard provided by the fire code in effect at time of inspection. The window shall be at least 5 square feet in total area, providing a clear opening of 24"H × 20"W, with the bottom of the opening not more than 44" above the floor except that one step or platform with a railing and permanently attached to the wall or floor and not more than 8" high may be allowed. A second door or stairway with a clear path to the outside is also required.

_____ 39. Minimum ceiling heights: Habitable rooms have a clear ceiling height over the minimum area required at not less than seven (7) feet, except that 1) in attics or top half-stories the ceiling height shall be not less than seven (7) feet over not less than one-third (1/3) of the minimum area required when used for sleeping, study, or similar activity: 2) in all spaces height may be reduced to 80" with adequate ventilation. In calculating the floor area of such rooms, only those portions of the floor area of the room having a clear ceiling height of five (5) feet or more may be included.

_____ 40. Water closet and lavatory: Every apartment shall contain within its walls a room separate from habitable rooms, which affords privacy and a water closet supplied with cold running water. The lavatory may be placed in the same room as the water closet, or, if located in another room, the lavatory shall be located in close proximity to the door leading directly into the room in which said water closet is located. The lavatory shall be supplied with hot and cold running water.

_____ 41. Bathtub or shower: Every apartment shall contain a room which affords privacy to a person in said room and which is equipped with a bathtub or shower supplied with hot and cold running water.

_____ 42. Kitchen sink: Every apartment shall contain a kitchen sink apart from the lavatory required under Item 42 and supplied with hot and cold running water.

_____ 43. General: Every sink, lavatory, bathtub or shower, drinking fountain, water closet or other facility shall be properly connected either to a public water system or to an approved private water system. All sinks, lavatories, bathtubs and showers shall be supplied with hot and cold running water.

_____ 44. Hot water heater: Every apartment shall be supplied with a separate hot water heater, or a single high capacity, fast recovery tank serving both units, capable of providing sufficient hot water (120 degrees F at the tap) during peak use.

_____ 45. General: Every sink, lavatory, bathtub or shower, drinking fountain, water closet or other facility shall be properly connected either to a public sewer system or to an approved private sewage disposal system.

_____ 46. Maintenance: Every plumbing stack and waste and sewer line shall be so installed and maintained as to function properly and shall be kept free from obstructions, leaks, and defects to prevent structural deterioration.

_____ 47. Every apartment shall be provided with heating facilities capable of maintaining a room temperature of sixty-eight (68) degrees F, at a point three (3) feet above the floor and three (3) feet from an exterior wall in all habitable rooms, bathrooms and toilet rooms. Each unit shall have a separate thermostat or other mechanism for independent control of the heat and temperature in that unit.

_____ 48. Cooking and heating equipment: All cooking and heating equipment, components, and accessories in every heating, cooking, and water heating device shall be maintained free from leaks and obstructions and kept functioning properly so as to be free from fire, health, and accident hazards. Portable cooking equipment employing flame is prohibited.

_____ 49. Kitchen facilities: Each unit must be equipped with a kitchen stove (top burners and oven) and a standard refrigerator plus shelves for dry food storage and adequate counter space for food preparation.

_____ 50. Fireplaces: Fireplaces, and other construction and devices intended for use similar to a fireplace, shall be stable and structurally safe and connected to approved chimneys.

_____ 51. Electrical service shall be adequate to carry computed load and shall be properly grounded.

_____ 52. Outlets required: Every habitable room shall contain at least two (2) separate and remote outlets, one (1) of which may be a ceiling or wall-type electric light fixture. In a kitchen, there must be a 20 amp circuit with three (3) separate and remote wall-type electric convenience outlets or two (2) such convenience outlets and one (1) ceiling or wall-type electric light fixture shall be provided. Every hall, bathroom, laundry room, or furnace room shall contain at least one (1) electric light fixture. In addition to the electric light fixture in every bathroom and laundry room, there shall be provided at least one (1) electric outlet. Outlets in bathrooms must be protected with ground fault connection interrupters.

_____ 53. Installation: All electrical equipment, wiring, and appliances shall be installed and maintained in a safe manner in accordance with all applicable laws. All electrical equipment shall be of an approved type.

_____ 54. Smoke detectors shall be installed in accordance with Fire Marshal's requirements.

_____ 55. A furnace or boiler shall not block the path of exit travel. When a furnace is so close to the line of exit travel that flames could block escape, a partial fire wall, at least 3′ from the furnace, may be used to protect the exit path.

_____ 56. There shall be no storage areas under stairways leading to or from the apartment.

_____ 57. That portion of the property not covered by parking spaces, structures, or appurtenances shall be maintained in accordance with applicable laws and regulations. In addition, these areas, when practical, shall be planted with grass or other ground cover, which shall be regularly cut or maintained. Bushes, trees, shrubbery, and other vegetation shall be properly maintained. In addition, appropriate measures to prevent soil erosion or gullying shall be established and maintained.

_____ 58. Exterior lighting must be provided at the outdoor entrance to the accessory apartment.

_____ 59. Parking area, driveway, and sidewalk surfaces shall be of a material which will assure a surface resistant to erosion.

_____ 60. All other conditions, as required by the grant of Special Exception by the Board.

=========== CHAPTER 4 ===========

ZONING

Finding Out About Zoning

Have you ever wondered who keeps a car wash from going in next door to you? Or why several homes in a prestigious residential neighborhood are not torn down to make way for an apartment building that would make enormous amounts of money for its owners? The answer is zoning.

Zoning classifies all the land in an entire city or town into land-use "zones." Generally speaking, within each zone only certain land uses are permitted. For example, only residential uses are permitted in residential zones, and only commercial uses in commercial zones. This enables all residents and business people to have an idea of what the area surrounding their home or business will look like in the future. It assures property owners of two things: that an annoying use will not be allowed next door and that their property values will remain stable.

Why Accessory Apartments Might Not Be Allowed in Your Neighborhood

Accessory apartments are often prohibited by zoning. Having someone else living in your home, especially when there is space available, doesn't seem likely to run down the neighborhood. In fact, it seems very unlikely that a small apartment could destroy a postwar neighborhood that withstood waves of baby boomers armed with drivers' licenses for dinosaurs on wheels.

Nonetheless, the zoning regulations of many communities make it illegal to install a separate apartment in a single-family home. In principle, these regulations attempt to thwart abuses that lower property values and downgrade the quality of the adjoining neighborhood. An unscrupulous investor could buy a home, put two rental units in it, and make a good income without maintaining the property well. This run-down house would make the adjoining houses less attractive to potential buyers. The owners of those houses would be losing money as the value of their homes dropped. In addition, while the unattractive house next door would make the homes hard to sell to most people, the low price would make them a good buy for an investor, perhaps the same one, who wanted to install another two apartments.

To prevent this kind of change in neighborhoods, traditional zoning laws prohibit accessory apartments. However, the dangers of poor maintenance and absentee landlords can be avoided by permitting accessory apartments under restricted conditions, such as only permitting homeowners to install them. Zoning provisions that protect neighborhoods are discussed below in the section "Advocating a Zoning Change." Properly regulated accessory apartments do not run down neighborhoods.

A variety of evidence shows that accessory apartments do not run down neighborhoods. The most convincing comes from looking at the two areas where accessory apartments seem to be most widespread. There are no good statistical data on how many people in what places have converted single-family homes, but the two places that appear to have gone furthest in changing zoning to permit accessory apartments are very affluent areas outside large cities. One is southwestern Connecticut, just northeast of New York City; it includes such towns as Westport, Greenwich, and Darien. The other is Marin County, California, outside San Francisco; it includes San Rafael and Mill Valley. These are not areas known for encouraging neighborhood decay.

Whom to Call for Information

Zoning laws are the responsibility of local government. The specific regulations that govern your property were approved by your local elected officials. These regulations are administered by the local planning or zoning office. Therefore, you should contact your local planning or zoning office to determine whether accessory apartments are a permitted use in your neighborhood.

Ask the official to read the regulations over the phone. You should start by asking what zone your home is in, and then ask to hear the regulations as they apply to that zone.

Be persistent when you call, because unless the ordinance has been changed recently, the official may not be immediately familiar with the details as they apply to your particular house and lot. There may be unique circumstances that apply to you. For example, if your home has enough land around it so that zoning would permit construction of two homes, it may be legal for you to install an accessory apartment. If you are in what is often called a rural or agricultural zone, it may be legal for you to have an accessory apartment. Many accessory apartment provisions in these zones were originally intended to provide housing for farm help. In addition, many towns near defense installations have zoning provisions dating from World War II that are designed to encourage subdivision of homes to provide housing for service personnel. These typically apply only to certain parts of the community.

In summary, persistence pays when dealing with your local planning and zoning officials. Whether accessory apartments are permitted in your zone or not, ask the official with whom you speak to send you a copy of the relevant portions of the ordinance. If the word is that they are not legal, you should double-check the regulations. If the word is that accessory apartments are legal, and you want to install an accessory apartment, you should have a copy to read when you have questions. Most towns that have recently changed their ordinances have an explanation sheet of some kind for homeowners.

Finally, in dealing with zoning officials, do not hesitate to ask for an explanation. You have probably heard and read endless references to the complexity of the modern world. Zoning ordinances are typically prize-winning examples of that complexity. Admire the local official for his or her understanding of such a complex subject, with sincerity, and then persist in requesting an explanation.

Waiting for a Zoning Change When Accessory Apartments Are Illegal

When most zoning laws were passed, accessory apartments were not exactly front-page news. That is not to say they were not around, just that no one called them accessory apartments or thought they were a very exciting idea. They were called mother-in-law apartments or single-family conversions. Zoning became widespread during the postwar building boom, and the focus then was on single-family homes for people starting families. The focus was first on starter homes, then on expandable homes, and then on convertible rec rooms, and nobody was much interested in the empty nester. Now the baby boomers of those years have left home and in doing so have created an empty nester boom made up of older Americans with too much housing and too little money. The baby boom has also produced a good many younger Americans with small households and small budgets. They grew up in middle-class suburban single-family-house neighborhoods and expect to go on living there. They need small apartments, either for themselves or as a source of income for their mortgage payments.

Politicians and planners realize that accessory apartments are a good fit in the housing market. That is why more and more communities are changing their zoning ordinances to permit accessory apartments. While there are no hard statistics, our estimate in 1984 suggested that they are legal in about 40 percent of the single-family neighborhoods in the country. But they are not legal everywhere.

The Likelihood of a Zoning Change

If accessory apartments are now illegal in your neighborhood, what does that mean for the future? What does it mean in terms of your hopes to install an accessory apartment? It means that you will have to do some political guesswork about how likely it is that the ordinance will be changed to permit accessory apartments in the near future. You will need to think about the attitude toward accessory apartments in your community. You can come up with a pretty good guess about how soon they might be permitted by getting the answers to the questions listed below. To get the answers you may have to make some phone calls to the planning office or to the office of an elected official.

Have the towns or counties next to yours changed zoning laws to allow for accessory apartments?

If adjoining jurisdictions are adopting accessory apartment ordinances, it is likely that your jurisdiction will follow.

Are accessory apartments being studied as a housing alternative by the planning office?

If accessory apartments are under study, then the wheels are turning toward adoption of an accessory apartment ordinance. If, however, the planning office is not studying accessory apartments, it is likely that they have not yet discovered their utility. Adoption in the near future is less likely.

Does the age of people in your community hint at a large group of persons that would be overhoused by the existing single-family-housing stock? Are there a lot of elderly people, single parents, and young families with few children?

If you have a large number of households in your community who could benefit from accessory apartments, then adoption of an accessory apartment ordinance is more likely.

Are there large numbers of existing illegal accessory apartments in your community?

If many illegal units already exist, there is probably growing pressure to clarify public policy about accessory apartments. Large numbers of illegal units can result in a health hazard because, without building inspections to enforce the building codes, the units are apt to be poorly installed. Clarifying public policy usually means legalizing accessory apartments because any other solution would mean displacement of too many people. Once the ordinance is passed, owners of illegal units are forced to bring their units up to code.

Do you think your neighbors would accept accessory apartments in your neighborhood?

As accessory apartment ordinances are adopted, the neighborhoods affected will voice their opinions in public hearings. Strong support for or against accessory apartments, as demonstrated by the residents and others, can significantly affect the adoption process.

Is the local Area Agency on Aging, or any other local aging advocacy group, interested in accessory apartments?

Leadership in efforts to change ordinances is often taken by aging advocates. If a major aging advocacy organization in your area is already interested in the idea, change may come rapidly.

If accessory apartment ordinances are already under study by your local government, it is possible the law will be in place by the time you are ready to start applying for a zoning permit. If the idea is barely on the drawing board, it may take a year or more for adoption of an ordinance. If no one is even thinking in terms of accessory apartments, you probably won't be able to install a legal unit for at least a couple of years.

Your local planning office is a good place to call to get answers to some of these questions. Another good place to call is your local Area Agency on Aging. The number can be obtained from telephone information if you can't find it in the directory. Often the agency will have another name, such as Commission of the Elderly or Department of Elder Affairs. Generally these agencies serve a large area, so if you live in a small town or county, you should call telephone information in the nearest large town or city.

The Cost of Waiting

Installing an accessory apartment may not be something you want to do right away. It may be an attractive alternative for the future, when one more kid is out of the nest or when you no longer use the rec room frequently. The time you would naturally wait may be the time needed for your community to adopt an accessory apartment ordinance. If you are interested, make sure that you advise your local politicians that you are in favor of their working toward adoption of an accessory apartment ordinance.

If you are eager to install an accessory apartment now, waiting can have serious drawbacks. Maybe the income is necessary if you are to retain your home in the wake of a divorce. Maybe the presence of another person around the house, especially one who might provide you with services, is essential if you are to continue living in your home. Or maybe you want the extra income so you can afford to put some money away for a trip next summer. Maybe you want to buy a house and install an accessory apartment to help pay the mortgage. If you think an accessory apartment could make your life better right now, the lack of an ordinance to permit it can be more than just a little frustrating.

You still have one alternative. It is not recommended by this book. On the other hand, it would not be responsible to readers not to discuss it. It is an alternative that is not only taken by many homeowners, but is quietly permitted by many local governments that simply look the other way. As one local planner put it, accessory apartments put planners between a rock and hard place. There were many illegal units in his community. He could not shut them down because too many people would be forced out of their homes. On the other hand, he did not feel he could get an ordinance passed to make them legal, because too many homeowners' associations would oppose legalization. Consequently he just looked the other way when illegal units were installed, so long as there were no complaints from the neighbors.

Installing an Apartment Illegally

If you have found out that accessory apartments are legal in your neighborhood, you can skip the rest of this chapter. If they are not legal, but you want to become involved in making them legal, skip this section and go on to the section of this chapter entitled "Advocating a Zoning Change." If, however, accessory apartments are illegal in your neighborhood and yet you believe it is important to you to install an accessory apartment now, what follows is worth reading.

If you do install an accessory apartment when it is not expressly permitted by the zoning ordinance, you will not be alone. Many homeowners who are considered good neighbors have installed apartments without any disturbance to their neighborhood. In fact, there may even be an accessory apartment on your block of which you are unaware. As noted earlier, a former head of the League of Women Voters of Westport, Connecticut, stated before her town's ordinance was approved, accessory apartments are "illegal, but not very illegal." Installing them where zoning does not permit them has been called the moral equivalent of jaywalking. Under the right circumstances, the risk is justified.

The Chances You Take

If accessory apartments are illegal and you choose to install one anyway, you will be breaking the law. There are penalties for doing so. Zoning is intended to protect the health, safety, and welfare of communities, and, as with any other law, there are consequences if you are caught violating it.

When installing an accessory apartment that is illegal, then, you also must consider the likelihood of getting caught, as well as whether anxiety about getting caught would be a problem for you. The history of most communities indicates that there is very little chance that you will be caught. But there are circumstances that increase the likelihood, and the consequences, of getting caught. Ask yourself the following questions:

Do the alterations require a building permit?

If you make sufficient alterations to need a building permit and have subsequent building inspections, the inspectors may notice that you are creating a separate living arrangement. This is especially true if they are inspecting hookups for a second kitchen or a new entrance. They are likely to guess what you are up to and ask you about it.

Does the local zoning enforcement officer take an active interest in finding illegal accessory apartments?

If your community has had no problems with accessory apartments in the past, it is doubtful that policing will occur. But if many complaints have been received about problem accessory apartments, policing efforts may be quite active. You can find out the situation in your community through a telephone call to the planning department. Also, your local newspaper may carry stories about illegal accessory apartments.

Would any of your neighbors become upset enough to report you to the zoning enforcement officer?

Are your neighbors inclined to watch closely what you do with your house? Would they be upset if you rented your apartment to someone? Have you ever had discussions with your neighbors about the idea of renting part of your home, in which they responded negatively? Has a neighbor ever rented part of his or her home and provoked unhappy responses from other neighbors? If you answered yes to any of these questions, you are probably treading on thin ice in terms of installing an illegal unit. Neighbors are often the most active zoning enforcement officers.

What will happen if you do get caught? What are the legal penalties? How much will you lose if you are forced to rip out your apartment?

Find out from the zoning regulations what the penalties are for having an illegal accessory apartment. In most cases the only requirement will be the removal of the accessory apartment. However, at least one county— Fairfax County, Virginia—used to have a provision in its zoning ordinance making the owner of an illegal unit liable for a fine of up to $1,000 per day while the unit was illegally rented. Accessory apartments are now legal in Fairfax County with certain restrictions.

Consider what will happen if you do install the apartment and are then forced by zoning enforcement to tear it out. If your apartment does not cost much to install, then being forced to close it down will not cost you much money. If you already have a rec room with a wet bar, a full bath, and a separate entrance, the installation will be inexpensive. You will not lose much if you are forced to close the apartment. In fact, you may make back in a couple of months' rent all that it cost you to install the apartment. On the other hand, if the apartment has been expensive to install, you will be risking a lot of money.

Another consideration is the potential public embarrassment of having the apartment closed down. At a minimum, your neighbors are likely to know you have been caught with an illegal apartment, and there may be newspaper articles. This is unlikely, but possible. It is more likely that, after a few years, an ordinance will be passed permitting accessory apartments and you will be able to legalize your apartment. When Babylon, New York, legalized accessory apartments, more than 700 homeowners came in to get their apartments legalized. In Montgomery County, Maryland, the figure was more than 200.

Would it be better to give up some privacy and take in a roomer rather than break the law?

You might get almost as much income, and you would avoid the complication of installing the apartment. This is an option many homeowners should consider.

The Ethics of Installing an Illegal Apartment

If you are going to install an accessory apartment that violates a zoning ordinance, you must feel comfortable with the idea. You might believe that you are just ahead in the zoning game, waiting for the local officials to catch up with progress. But on the other hand, it might be contrary to your moral character to do something that is officially disallowed. Recognizing how you feel about installing an illegal apartment is the major key to whether or not you should. You will be breaking the law, and clearly just because many people do it does not justify another person's doing it.

If you think laws against accessory apartments do not make sense, you should remember that there are likewise laws that you feel protect you. You would not take kindly to those laws being disregarded by others who may not agree. Ethically, your individual need for the apartment, and the particular combination of income, security, companionship, and other benefits it may bring you, must be substantial to justify violating zoning.

Do your circumstances justify your breaking the law, albeit a minor one? There are probably at least two cases where many reasonable people would agree they do. One is the case of a recently divorced single parent who may lose his or her house without the income of an accessory apartment. The other is the case of an older person who may be forced to leave a long-term home without the income and other benefits of an accessory apartment. There are other individual circumstances that would justify an illegal apartment, as well as many that would not.

Advocating a Zoning Change

If your circumstances permit, a good alternative to an illegal apartment is waiting and working to make accessory apartments legal. If zoning ordinances in your community have not been changed to allow for accessory apartments, you can play a part in advocating that change.

In 1980, the town of Babylon, New York, legalized accessory apartments and became the first community to receive significant public attention for doing so. Now state laws effectively legalizing accessory apartments have been passed in Hawaii and California, and innumerable towns and counties across the country have also amended their zoning. The efforts stem from a variety of sources, but the major cause of the changes is the appeal of the simple logic of providing homeowners with extra income while creating inexpensive new housing.

Voicing Your Interests

Who has the power to make accessory apartments legal in your community? It varies from community to community, depending on how much power has been delegated by your community's legislative body to its planning and zoning commission. In most cases, either the legislative body or the planning and zoning commission could initiate the change to permit accessory apartments. Also, in most cases, neither body will act on an amendment without some consultation with the other. Assuming, then, as the rest of this chapter does, that you are interested in trying to get accessory apartments legalized, the people on your town or county council and on your planning and zoning commission are the people you have to get to. There are, however, two other groups you should also consider. Those are your local housing commission and the commission on aging, assuming they exist.

Remember that your local officials are elected or appointed to both lead and represent your community. If they think that an accessory apartment ordinance is the desire of the community, they will also feel to some extent obliged to represent you accordingly, particularly if they want to be reelected. For some, leadership may mean leading the fight against an ordinance change, but in most communities the opposition has not been successful.

The time when voicing your interests will be most effective is during a public hearing on accessory apartments. Accessory apartment ordinances are difficult to pass unless concerned citizens speak from their hearts at the hearing. If you or others can speak to the point that installation of an accessory apartment is the only way for you to keep your home, you will be providing the type of testimony that tends to sway politicians.

Being Patient

As you go about your advocacy work, above all *be patient*. . . .Like a fox. Any change that comes through the political process is slow, because what is self-evident to one side is often not at all self-evident to the other. Politicians are caught in the middle and have to tiptoe through the land mines that people on either side of any issue have laid down. As a result, tiptoeing toward change is inherent in our democratic system.

It is also important to realize that accessory apartments are a radical change to zoning ordinances. They introduce a flexibility to single-family zoning that has no precedent. Politicians will act cautiously because they are uncertain as to how accessory apartments will affect single-family neighborhoods. Similarly some homeowners' associations, out of their fear of the unknown, are more comfortable saying no at first.

Have some respect for the opposition. A single-family home is most families' largest financial asset, and the quality of the neighborhood it is located in is probably as important as any other factor in the quality of a family's life. When you suggest changing zoning, you are suggesting changing the laws that many people see as basic protection for both their financial security and the quality of their environment. You are suggesting changes in the basic underpinnings of their lives. Do not be surprised, then, if they react with skepticism and caution.

On the other hand, don't let the opposition's skepticism and caution dissuade you. National experience with adoption of accessory apartments indicates that fears of change in single-family neighborhoods are un- founded. Passage of accessory apartment ordinances in Falls Church, Virginia, and Montgomery County, Maryland, in 1983 resulted in only a handful of applications for new apartments through 1985. Many com- munities have found it necessary to encourage installations of accessory apartments after the ordinance was in place. Overwhelming changes are not likely.

In some communities there has been opposition to accessory apart- ments on the grounds that they were running down the neighborhood. An example is Takoma Park, Maryland. However, in most such cases, the neighborhood was already being run down due to a poor market for home sales, and the protest was by a new generation of homebuyers trying to upgrade the neighborhood and get rid of investor-owners. Apartments in such neighborhoods have often been installed illegally by absentee investor-owners; apartments in homes where the homeowner lives typi- cally are much more acceptable. Also, in such neighborhoods even those opposing accessory apartments generally recognize that without the in- come from the apartments many homes would have become more run- down.

Volunteering Your Time

Any undertaking to alter current laws will require time from volunteers. Are you willing to give up some of your spare time for this effort? You might be compensated in that you clear up the legality of installing an accessory apartment in your own home. You might also get some satisfaction from doing something that not only benefits you, but will also benefit others in similar situations.

Forming Coalitions

This is where the fox part comes in. It is doubtful that you would want to take on the campaign for adopting an accessory apartment ordinance on your own. However, it is likely that a variety of community groups could take on the responsibility of this type of campaign. You might play a role in getting accessory apartments on the agenda of one of these groups. In addition, you might play a role in bringing together interest groups that benefit from accessory apartment ordinances. Forming a coalition, a group of interest groups, increases the power base and the chances of getting the zoning changed. Some likely groups are listed below.

The Elderly. They can turn their empty rooms into a source of income, security, companionship, and possible services in exchange for a reduction in rent. Contact your local commission on aging (which may also be known as the Area Agency on Aging), chapters of the American Association of Retired Persons, the Gray Panthers, or any other aging advocacy organization.

Single Parents. Parents who find themselves suddenly single through death or divorce can rent out their rooms as a way of keeping their homes and keeping their children in neighborhoods they might otherwise be forced to leave. Contact a local chapter of Parents Without Partners or any other group concerned with the problems of single parents.

Young Housebuyers. They can rent out rooms as apartments, enabling them to buy homes now and expand into them as their incomes and families grow. Contact large employers known to be recruiting young professionals to move into the area. The best way to find out about such corporations is through your local economic development commission or chamber of commerce.

Homebuilders. Accessory apartments represent a means to build affordable new homes without negotiating for a rollback of zoning standards. Homes with built-in accessory apartments can be sold to a much broader spectrum of the housing market. Contact your local Homebuilders Association.

Remodelers. Installing accessory apartments means work for the remodeling industry. Contact the Remodelers Council of your local Homebuilders Association.

Real Estate Agents. Accessory apartments provide another way to help make a house affordable to a young couple. In addition, real estate agents can often make money managing accessory apartments for homeowners. Contact your local Board of Realtors.

Savings and Loan Institutions. They can profit by the increased use of loan money for remodeling purposes. Contact a local association of savings and loans.

Hospitals. Older people are often hospitalized prematurely or discharged late because they live alone. Accessory apartments can reduce the frequency with which this occurs. Contact discharge planners at your local hospital.

Dealing with Homeowners' Association Opposition

Often people will respond to new ideas with a "no." They feel that if you don't know, vote no. This is likely to be the response of homeowners' associations to accessory apartments. They are not sure if allowing accessory apartments into their neighborhood will change its quality, and they do not want to take the risk of finding out. But—and here is where you gather your ammunition—isn't that stance unrepresentative of many of their members? Aren't the elderly, single parents, and young families also homeowners? If you want to temper the attack on accessory apartments from homeowners' associations, then, ask some pointed questions. The best place to ask these is in a public hearing, but it is always good to practice first. Call up a public official or the head of a civic association who opposes accessory apartments and put some of the following questions to him or her:

1. Have you talked to your elderly constituents? If so, did the ones you talked to have any experience with accessory apartments?

2. Have you ever talked to anyone who had an accessory apartment? Did it help them much?

3. You say zoning is supposed to protect long-term neighborhood residents. Is it protecting long-term residents to force them to give up their homes because they cannot get the income and security they need from an accessory apartment?

4. Have you talked to single parents? Do you think it would help a single parent to be able to install an accessory apartment? Do you think many have to sell their homes because they can't install an accessory apartment?

5. You say accessory apartments will run down neighborhoods. Have you checked on how many illegal ones we have already? Are they running down neighborhoods? Can you give me any examples of accessory apartments running down neighborhoods where the running down wasn't actually being done by other housing market forces?

6. You say there will be problems with maintenance. Don't more problems with maintenance come from older homeowners who can't maintain their homes themselves and don't have the income to get someone to help them? Wouldn't that situation be improved by accessory apartments?

7. Have you considered how an accessory apartment ordinance would allow young people to buy in the neighborhood?

8. How many accessory apartments do you think would be installed following the passage of an ordinance permitting them? Assuming there will not be a large number, would you still oppose an ordinance?

Getting the Materials You Need

If you are going to be actively involved in the advocacy of accessory apartments, it is important for you to read up-to-date information on the subject. One source is the American Association of Retired Persons, which offers a variety of free materials on the benefit of accessory apartments for the elderly. Another is the American Planning Association, which has a publication specifically on accessory apartment ordinances.

Finally, Patrick H. Hare Planning and Design offers a variety of technical materials on the subject of accessory apartments. Addresses are as follows:

For free materials from the American Association of Retired Persons, write or call requesting materials on accessory apartments:

> Housing Coordinator
> AARP
> 1909 K Street, NW
> Washington, DC 20049
> (202)728-4396

For material on zoning ordinances, send $10.00 and a letter requesting PAS Report No. 365, *Accessory Apartments: Using the Surplus Space in Single Family Homes*, to:

> Planner's Bookshop
> American Planning Association
> 1313 East 60th Street
> Chicago, IL 60637

For a free list of materials on promoting accessory apartments and other alternative living arrangements, send a self-addressed, stamped envelope to:

> Patrick H. Hare Planning and Design
> 1246 Monroe Street, NE
> Washington, DC 20017

What You Should Know About Zoning for Accessory Apartments

The booklet listed above from the American Planning Association gives a good description of what a zoning ordinance permitting accessory apartments should include. It is too detailed to cover completely here. However, you should know the basic provisions that are included in most amendments to permit accessory apartments that are now being passed. In addition, there are two new ones of which you should also be aware. These basic provisions are listed below, with some explanation.

Accessory apartments should be allowed as a special exception with an annual or biennial renewal.

Most zoning is "as of right." That means that if zoning permits you to do something, you have the right to do it without meeting additional conditions. A special exception use requires you to apply for a conditional permit, and additional restrictions, generally spelled out in the ordinance, can be placed on you. In addition, renewal of the permit can be required, and the opportunity to apply for a special exception can be withdrawn. In general, this reassures communities that apartments can be restricted or limited if too many are installed or if reasonable new restrictions on them are suggested by neighbors or other interested parties.

Only homeowners should be allowed to install accessory apartments.

As discussed earlier, one of the main concerns about accessory apartments is how well they will be maintained. In addition, the intention of most ordinances is to benefit existing owners, not investment owners. For both of these reasons, the opportunity to install accessory apartments is limited to homeowners who live in the home where the accessory apartment is going to be installed. It is generally assumed that a homeowner who lives next door to his or her tenant will be very careful about who the tenants are and how they behave. In addition, homeowners are likely to be very careful about how the exterior of an accessory apartment looks if it is part of their home.

Some ordinances restrict new buyers from installing an apartment until they have lived in their homes for one or more years. These restrictions frustrate new homebuyers who need the rental income from an apartment to make a house affordable.

Changes to the exterior of the original home should be minimized.

Beauty is in the eye of the beholder. The logic of this provision is that if the beholder doesn't know accessory apartments are present, neighborhoods will be more beautiful. At a minimum, advocates of accessory apartments do not want to be put in the position of advocating gaunt exterior stairways, or garage doors that have air conditioners sticking through them. The purpose of this provision is to minimize exterior change in the neighborhood.

Accessory apartments should not be concentrated in specific areas.

This is a new provision that is not in most of the literature on accessory apartments. It speaks directly to fears that many of the homes in an area may be converted. Experience indicates that this is very rare except where a developer has built a subdivision of homes that all have the same house plan, and it happens to be a plan that converts very easily. The provision was developed first by Boulder, Colorado. It specifies that no more than 10 percent of the homes whose lots are within 300 feet of the owner who wants an accessory apartment can already have apartments installed in them. If the 10 percent figure is exceeded, the applicant's request for a permit to install an accessory apartment is denied. This provision ensures that no neighborhood will develop an excessive concentration of accessory apartments. It is a good provision because it reassures many of those opposed to accessory apartments. Besides, it can always be changed once experience has shown that accessory apartments do not harm neighborhoods.

Zoning enforcement officers should send abutting neighbors self-addressed, stamped comment cards before the annual or biennial renewal of accessory apartment permits.

Opponents of accessory apartments worry about enforcement of the zoning ordinance and about how the apartments will be managed and maintained. They ask for more zoning enforcement. In practice, very few local governments have enough time to go around looking for zoning violations. They investigate complaints. In other words, zoning enforcement takes place by complaint. This provision simply recognizes that fact and creates a mechanism to make complaints easier to submit. It strengthens enforcement at very low cost to local government. This provision has been part of numerous discussions on accessory apartment ordinances. At present, however, it does not appear to have been used by any local governments.

There are numerous other provisions of nearly equal importance that should be in an ordinance permitting accessory apartments. The best source for familiarizing yourself with them is the booklet listed above that is published by the American Planning Association.

CHAPTER 5

HOW WILL AN ACCESSORY APARTMENT AFFECT YOUR TAXES?

This chapter looks at taxes from several angles. It considers property taxes, which will probably go up a little with the installation of an accessory apartment. It considers how you can deduct expenses related to the apartment. It discusses the fact that if you receive services in place of rent you have to report them as income. Finally, it looks at the substantial tax benefits you gain from being able to depreciate the apartment.

You should realize that there are many gray areas in the tax code and accessory apartments is one such area. The information in this chapter is a compilation of pieces drawn from various IRS publications on rental property, appreciation, and other subjects that logically apply to accessory apartments. This information is given as general guidance and you may want to check with a tax specialist when you prepare your tax return, especially the first year you have an apartment. References in this chapter to IRS publications are up-to-date for 1985 tax returns. You should check for changes for the current tax year. As this book goes to press, Congress is considering tax legislation.

Will There Be a Great Increase in Property Tax?

Adding an accessory apartment to your home will require some remodeling. You might be adding a kitchen or a bathroom. You might be taking space used for storage, such as an attic, and turning it into livable space. These additions are improving your property. You can expect the market value of your home to increase roughly by the amount you spend creating the apartment.

For tax purposes, the local tax department estimates the market value of your property. Your property tax is a percentage of that value. The local tax department typically sends tax assessors to reassess the value of homes whenever a building permit has been granted. In other words, applying for a building permit for an accessory apartment will trigger a new assessment in most communities.

Since the accessory apartment increases the value of your home, you can also expect it to increase your property tax. Don't let that worry you, however, because the amount will not be that great. A survey of towns with accessory apartments, by city planner Rita Calvan, supports the idea that property tax increases for homes with accessory apartments are generally small. A summary of her findings states:

> Although homeowners are correct when they assume that their property will be reassessed for tax purposes upon conversion, the actual amount of a tax increase is usually rather small. (Respondents reported a dollar increase of between $15 and $700, with the average being $24.)
>
> In a related finding, respondents reported that the knowledge or belief that their property taxes will increase does not usually dissuade homeowners from installing accessory dwellings. Compared to the cost of conversion or to the new income an accessory unit may bring, the property tax is a relatively small burden. Thus, it probably weighs proportionately less among the total number of factors which must be considered in deciding whether to convert an existing home. Moreover, where the tax burden can be shifted forward to renters of an accessory unit, a homeowner will bear little of the burden of higher taxes. (From "Are Property Values

and Taxes Affected by the Home Conversion? *Realtor Magazine*
[published by the Washington Area Board of Realtors], November
1984.)

Is Rent Considered Taxable Income?

The money you receive as rent is considered income by the Internal
Revenue Service, but before you tack the amount onto your taxable
income, you can deduct your expenses from it. As discussed below, you
will probably find enough expenses to deduct so that your taxable income
from rent is zero or very close to it.

The IRS also gives instructions on how to treat security deposits
received from your tenant. For example, you might require your tenant
to pay advance rent to cover the last month's rent. This advance rent will
be counted as income in the year you receive it, regardless of the date
of the last month of occupancy. Or, you might require a security deposit
from your tenant. If you plan to return the deposit at the end of the
tenant's occupancy, you will not count the deposit as income.

Are Services Provided in Place of Rent Considered Taxable Income?

Suppose you and your tenant have agreed that your tenant will provide
a particular service in full or partial payment of the rent. Maybe the
tenant will do all yard work for a $150 rent reduction. This service is
counted as income by the IRS just as if it were rental dollars. So in this
case the service of yard work is equal to $150. Let's say the tenant pays
an additional $200 as rent. You would report $350 as your rental income.

How will you put a dollar value on the service(s) exchanged? The
IRS requires that you estimate the fair market value of the service, that
is, how much you would be charged by an agency offering that service.
On the other hand, the IRS also says that "if the services were rendered
at a stipulated price, such price will be presumed to be the fair market
value of the compensation in the absence of evidence to the contrary."
In practice, the rent reduction will almost always be far less than what
it would cost the homeowner to get the same service elsewhere.

The reason for this difference is that as a homeowner with an accessory apartment, you and your tenant have created your own little market simply by living side by side. Suppose the tenant does yard work for you. Living next to you, he or she has no travel costs. Similarly, the tenant is likely to use your yard tools and lawn mower. Unlike a landscaping and gardening service, the tenant does not have to have a secretary to answer calls, or a phone, or an office, or a pickup truck. In fact, the tenant has no overhead to pay for at all. In summary, the tenant, without travel costs or overhead, can charge much less than a landscaping service. The fact that the professional landscaping service cannot compete with a tenant in price does not mean that the tenant's services are being undervalued for income tax purposes. It simply means that you and your tenant bargain in the context of a very local market with its own "fair market values."

In summary, in estimating the value of services provided in return for rent reductions, all you have to ask yourself is, "How much have I reduced the rent in exchange for the service?" This dollar amount should be treated as income. In case you need additional explanation, included as Appendix 1 is the IRS's detailed explanation of how to treat compensation for services.

Can Expenses Related to the Apartment Be Deducted?

You Can Keep All the Deductions You Had Before the Apartment

As a homeowner, you qualify for certain income tax deductions. IRS Publication No. 530, *Tax Information for Homeowners*, explains which costs of acquiring your home are deductible from your income tax. The most typical and advantageous deductions are for mortgage interest payments and property tax payments. It is likely that you are familiar with itemizing to claim these deductions. The addition of the accessory apartment will not change those benefits that you may now receive from home ownership.

You Will Gain Deductions as an Owner of Rental Property

As an owner of rental property you qualify for new deductions. These go beyond any deductions you receive as a homeowner. First, you can deduct interest payments on your remodeling loan. Second, you can deduct operating expenses. Third, you can deduct depreciation of the rental unit. And finally, you can deduct for depreciation of any furniture or appliances you provide in the rental unit. Let's look at these new tax deductions individually.

Interest Payments on Remodeling Loan

You will probably borrow money to pay for installing the accessory apartment. As you pay off the loan, the first monthly payments you make will be mostly payments of interest, with very little principal. All the money you pay in interest can be deducted from your taxable income.

Deduction of Rental Expenses

You are also allowed deductions for the costs of operating the rental unit. These expenses are of three types: repairs, insurance premiums, and charges for services. First, look at repairs. For tax purposes, a repair must be distinguished from an improvement. A repair to the accessory apartment is deductible from the rental income, but an improvement is not. An improvement still affects your taxes because, like any investment in residential property for rent, you can depreciate it. Depreciation will be discussed in detail later in this chapter because it is handled differently than operating expenses. As defined by the IRS, "a repair keeps your property in good operating condition. It does not materially add to the value of your property or substantially prolong its life."

The second type of operating expense is monthly insurance premiums. If you have insurance covering the apartment, the premium can be deducted from your rental income.

Finally, you can deduct charges for services. Will you be paying for services such as water, sewer, trash collection, or heating and cooling? If you will be, you have another tax deduction.

However, you may also have another complication as well. The bills for services, as well as the bills for insurance and repairs, will frequently cover both the portion of the house the owner inhabits and the accessory apartment. You can deduct only the portions of these bills that service the apartment. An example of how to divide expenses, from IRS Publication No. 527, *Rental Property*, is given below.

Dividing Expenses

If an expense is for both rental use and personal use, such as heat for the entire house or mortgage interest, you must divide the expense between rental use and personal use. You may use any reasonable method for dividing the expenses. The two most common methods are one based on the number of rooms in your home and one based on area.

Example

You rent a room in your house. The room is 12 × 15 feet, or 180 square feet. Your entire house has 1,800 square feet of floor space. You may deduct as rental expense 10% of any expense that must be divided between rental use and personal use. Thus, if your heating bill for the year for the entire house was $600, $60 ($600 × 10%) is a rental expense. The balance, $540, is a personal expense and you may not deduct it.

Some readers may want to obtain the full text of the IRS pamphlet from which the example is taken, or other relevant IRS publications mentioned below. They should be ordered by number from the IRS Forms Distribution Center. Phone, toll-free, (800) 424-FORM during business hours.

Depreciation of the Rental Unit

This tax deduction can offer the largest break to the rental unit owner. The deduction reflects the wear and tear and aging of the rental unit. In effect, it says you can deduct from your income the value you have lost through wear and tear on the apartment each year. Obviously, you can only "depreciate," or deduct from your income, the portion of your home that comprises the accessory apartment. You cannot depreciate the portion of your home used for your own personal purposes. As explained later in the examples, the value of the accessory apartment from which yearly depreciation figures are calculated has two parts: first, the portion of your home that is used for the apartment, and second, the money you invest in creating the apartment.

Depreciation of Furnishings Used in the Rental Unit

Because the accessory apartment is income-producing property, you are also allowed to depreciate any furnishings you supply for the unit. Suppose you leave a guest bedroom set in what is now the bedroom of the apartment, or suppose you buy a refrigerator for the new kitchen. Since you are not using this property personally but are instead using it in your "rental business," you will be able to deduct depreciation for the bedroom set or the refrigerator. According to the IRS, the furnishings "must have a determinable life and that life must be longer than one year" and "must be something that wears out, decays, gets used up, becomes obsolete, or loses value from natural causes" (IRS Publication No. 534, *Depreciation*, p. 1). In other words, suppose you put an accessory apartment in part of your house and have some extra furniture that's in good condition and not needed. Furnishing the apartment with it might add a little to how much you make off the apartment.

Another possibility is to buy new appliances for your own home and put your older ones, which are still in good condition, in the apartment. You will get the benefit of new appliances and still get some of the benefits of depreciation.

As an aside, you must be careful not to depreciate appliances, such as a refrigerator, if they have already been included in the value of the rental unit itself. In general, you will recover your money outlay more readily through depreciating appliances as furnishings rather than as part of the rental unit.

Calculating Depreciation

The IRS established a handful of depreciation methods which are still in use, but which are being replaced by the accelerated cost recovery system (ACRS). The critical factor in determining which depreciation method to use depends on the year in which your property was purchased. All property purchased prior to January 1, 1981, must be depreciated using one of the older IRS methods, such as the straight-line method. All property purchased in 1981 or later must use the ACRS.

The Straight-Line Method

As noted above, the straight-line method is only one of several methods you can use to depreciate property purchased before 1981. However, it is the simplest to understand because it allows for equal deductions each year. Once you understand it, you will feel comfortable with other methods of depreciation which allow greater deductions in your first years of renting the apartment. These methods, as well as the straight-line method, are described in IRS Publication No. 534, *Depreciation*.

How do you calculate the annual deduction you are allowed for depreciation under the straight-line method? First, you need to come up with three figures: the basis of the property, the salvage value, and the useful life of the property.

Calculating the Basis of the Property

The basis of the property is that part of the total value of the property that is eligible for depreciation. Since you can depreciate only the rental unit, you must calculate the value of the unit apart from the rest of your home and the value of the land it is built on. That amount is called the basis of the property eligible for depreciation.

To start with, the value of your entire home must be determined. The IRS requires you to use the lesser of its fair market value or its "adjusted basis." If you find it confusing that the IRS is using the adjusted basis as the basis for the basis, so do many other people.

A quick way to estimate the fair market value of your home is to call a local real estate agent. To determine the adjusted basis of the property, take the original cost of the property when you bought it; to that figure add the cost of any improvements and subtract the cost of any casualty losses claimed during earlier tax years. The result is your adjusted basis. Compare it to the fair market value. The lesser of the two is the value of your entire property according to the IRS and will be used to calculate the basis of the property.

The next step is to separate the contributions the house and the lot make to the value of the entire property. According to the IRS, "if no better evidence is available, you may use the assessed values of land and improvements when you got your property to determine the relative values of the building and the lot." "Improvements" in this case means improvements on your land—that is, your home. To find out these assessed values at the time of your purchase, if you no longer have records, call the tax assessor's office in your community.

When you have just the value of your house, multiply it by the percentage of the home used for the rental apartment. In other words, estimate the size or square footage of the part of the original house you will be using for the apartment. Divide it by the size or square footage of the house itself to get the percentage of the home used for the apartment. Expressed as a formula, the dollar amount of the home used for the apartment equals

$$
\left[\begin{array}{l} \text{Lesser of fair} \\ \text{market value} \\ \text{or adjusted} \\ \text{basis} \end{array} - \begin{array}{l} \text{Value of} \\ \text{land} \end{array} \right] \times \begin{array}{c} \text{Percent of} \\ \text{house used as} \\ \text{apartment} \end{array} = \begin{array}{c} \text{Dollar value of} \\ \text{part of home} \\ \text{used for apart-} \\ \text{ment} \end{array}
$$

Now, to get the basis of the property eligible for depreciation, take the dollar value of the part of the home used for the apartment and add the cost of installing the apartment. In other words, once you have found the value of the floor area of the apartment you should add the construction costs of installing the apartment. If some of the construction costs are for improvements made to the part of the house you will continue to use, they must be excluded. The formula is

$$
\begin{array}{c} \text{Dollar value of} \\ \text{part of home used} \\ \text{for apartment} \end{array} + \begin{array}{c} \text{Cost of improve-} \\ \text{ments to create} \\ \text{apartment} \end{array} = \begin{array}{c} \text{Basis of property} \\ \text{eligible for} \\ \text{depreciation} \end{array}
$$

For further clarification, sections of the IRS discussions of these issues are included in Appendixes 2 and 3 under the titles "Renting Part of Your Property" and "Property Changed to Rental Use." These are from IRS Publication No. 527, *Rental Property.*

Calculating the Useful Life of the Property

The second of the three figures you need to calculate is the useful life of the property. It is the number of years you can reasonably expect to use your property. No average useful life for homes is assigned by the IRS. In its simplest sense, it is an estimate of the length of time before the house will fall apart. You are not likely to let the house fall apart anyway, and therefore its life is indefinite. The IRS is asking you to theorize about something that probably will not happen. In Appendix 4 you will find the IRS discussion of calculating the useful life of your property. It is not very helpful.

This is one of those situations where it is best to apply a rule of thumb. The rule of thumb to apply here is that the useful life of your house is about as long as the mortgage a bank would give on it to a new buyer. In most cases today, that will be 30 years. In other words, you are saying that if the banks won't bet that your property will last more than 30 years, why should you or the IRS?

As an aside, it's in your interest to propose a "useful life" that is reasonable but not overly long. A very long life would result in a very small amount of annual depreciation, and therefore an equally small tax deduction for you.

Calculating the Salvage Value of the Property

The third of the three figures you need to estimate depreciation is salvage value. It is the expected selling price at the end of the property's useful life—or, in other words, how much you would be able to sell your home for once it fell apart. More on salvage value from the IRS is in Appendix 5. Here the IRS discussion is a little more useful.

It is important to note that the IRS talks not only about salvage value but also about net salvage value. That is what you would have in your theoretical pocket after you had paid someone to take away the value-less rubble of your no-longer-useful home. In almost all cases it will cost more to haul away the rubble of a house than the salvage value of the materials. Accordingly, for most people, the salvage value of their homes will be zero, since the IRS does not let you have negative net salvage.

Using the Formula

Now you are ready to plug the three figures into the straight-line method formula. Take the basis of the property, subtract the salvage value, and divide by the useful life of the property.

$$\frac{\text{Basis of the property} - \text{Salvage value}}{\text{Useful life of the property}} = \text{Annual deduction}$$

The figure you calculate is the actual dollar amount of depreciation you can deduct each year. The last section of this chapter explains how to report depreciation to the IRS.

Remember that you can also depreciate any personal property used in the apartment, such as furniture and appliances. In doing so you also use the straight-line method, or one of its cousins, if the items were purchased before 1981. The basis of the personal property is its current market value, the useful life is how long you expect to use the item in the apartment, and the salvage value is the resale value at the end of the useful life.

The Accelerated Cost Recovery System

The accelerated cost recovery system (ACRS) is the chief depreciation system now in use by the IRS. It allows you larger deductions early on in your "rental business." Since it is likely that at least some of the furniture and appliances you use in the apartment will have been purchased since 1980, the ACRS is applicable to them. If you have purchased your home since December 31, 1980, you must depreciate the rental unit using ACRS. If you owned it before that date, but are installing the apartment now, you cannot use ACRS. Also, if a relative owned the property in 1980, or if you lease the apartment back to its 1980 owner or a relative of that owner, you cannot use ACRS.

Calculating the Unadjusted Basis of the Property Under ACRS

First, consider furnishings. The basis of property bought new is the purchase price. For property bought used, the basis is the purchase price plus the cost of any reconditioning you do at the time of purchase. If you buy a new refrigerator for the apartment at a cost of $600, the basis is $600. If you buy a used bedroom set for $150 and refinish it at a cost of $25, the basis is $175.

If you are depreciating your own used furnishings in the apartment, use the current resale value as the basis. However, if you bought these furnishings before 1981, they cannot be depreciated using ACRS. Instead, use one of the methods, such as straight-line, that predates ACRS.

In the case of a home, the basis of the property is figured the same way as in the straight-line method example. You take the cost of the property, subtract the cost of the land, multiply by the percentage of space occupied by the apartment, and add the cost of improvements.

Determining the Class of the Property

Under ACRS, anything to be depreciated is classified according to how long it can typically be expected to last. Furniture and appliances, the items you are most likely to be depreciating in the apartment, are classified as 5-year property. Each class of property is depreciated by a different percentage each year according to a table provided by the IRS. For 5-year property, the table is as follows:

1st year	15%
2nd year	22%
3rd year	21%
4th year	21%
5th year	21%
	100%

If you depreciate your home, it is classified as 15- or 18- or 19-year property, depending on when you purchased it. Homes purchased between January 1, 1981, and March 15, 1984 (inclusive), are classified as 15-year property. Homes purchased after March 15, 1984, and before May 9, 1985, are classified as 18-year property. Homes purchased on or after May 9, 1985, are classified as 19-year property. (The reason for all of the shifting is that Congress cannot decide on the appropriate length of the recovery period for real property. The percentages for these recovery periods are assigned according to the *month* and year you install the apartment. (See how the IRS thinks ahead to make it no more advantageous to buy something at the end of the year than at the beginning of the year.) A copy of the 15- and 18-year tables is found in Appendix 6.

Calculating the Dollar Amount of the Deduction

Multiply the basis of the property by the percentage derived from the table. For example, during the first year you could deduct $26.25 (15 percent of $175) for the bedroom set and $60 (15 percent of $400) for the refrigerator. Or in the case of your apartment classified as 15-year property and installed in January, you could deduct 12 percent of the value of the apartment or 1 percent per month.

How to Report Your Rental Income and Expenses

You are required to use Schedule E, Part I, to report rental income and expenses. You may want to follow along with the Schedule E form reprinted in Appendix 7 as you read these instructions. First, list on the form the total rent you received. Then, prepare the total of the rental expenses by listing each expense separately and then totaling them. Next, add the depreciation deduction to the expense total. You should now have two figures: the total income and total expense figures. Compare the two. If the total income is larger than the total expense, you have a profit. If the total expense is larger than the total income, you have a loss. The plus or minus amount will be transferred to your main tax form, the 1040. Detailed instructions for completing this form are found in the 1040 instruction booklet.

You may have wondered, in reading the above, whether there is an IRS form for calculating the depreciation figure. Yes, there is. Form 4562 is where you figure depreciation for the apartment itself and any other depreciable items used in the apartment. You can see an example in Appendix 8. Use Section B to list recovery property, which is property purchased after December 31, 1980, and depreciated according to ACRS. Then use Section C to list nonrecovery property, which is property purchased before January 1, 1981, and depreciated according to the straight-line method. The amounts for each section are totaled, and this is the figure used on Schedule E. The IRS also provides an instruction sheet for completing Form 4562.

These tax forms will look clear to you if you see them as a big fish eating a little fish which has eaten an even smaller fish. The Form 1040 that everyone files feeds off the figure calculated on Schedule E, the rental income and expenses. Schedule E, in turn, feeds off the figure calculated on Form 4562, for depreciation.

Two Final Points

Recapture

Remember that depreciation is basically a way of deferring taxation. When you go to sell your property, the tax benefits you have gotten from depreciation will increase what the IRS considers to be gain, or profit. Your taxes on the sale will increase. Since you have depreciated part of the home, more of your sales price is considered profit. Generally, that profit stemming from depreciation will be taxed as ordinary income.

In other words, the benefits of depreciation have some serious strings attached. In most cases, however, they will still be benefits. To most people, money now is better than money later. Tax planning, however, is something you should think about. Consider when you might sell your house. Will your tax bracket be higher than it is now? If so, you should probably talk to a tax specialist. The section on "Selling Rental Property" in the back of IRS Publication No. 527 gives more details. It should be noted that under certain conditions, owners over 55 selling property used in part for rent do not have to report any of the gain as ordinary income. Again, a tax specialist should be consulted.

Depreciation and Renting to Relatives

In many cases, accessory apartments are installed for relatives. This raises the question of whether or not the owner of the home can take depreciation in such cases. The answer is almost always yes, if the relative is being charged a fair market rent.

CHAPTER 6

COSTS AND FINANCING THE APARTMENT

Estimating the Costs of Installation

The typical cost for an accessory apartment is $16,500. Your apartment might cost more, but it also might cost a great deal less. Two principal factors determine the cost: how simply your home can be converted and how much of the remodeling work you do yourself. You cannot assume it will cost the "typical" amount to install an apartment in your home.

First, think about the design of your home. The less you have to change your home to make the apartment, the lower the cost. In general, if the space you are converting is finished, habitable space, it can be converted easily. An example is a finished basement area or rec room with a full bathroom and plenty of light. In contrast, garages and attics normally require that you make them livable and are accordingly harder to convert.

The cost of installing an accessory apartment will also be increased greatly if you need to install a separate entrance. A walk-out basement requires little, if any, remodeling to make a separate entrance. On the

other hand, an attic or second-floor conversion might require a recon-
struction of the existing stairs, or construction of an exterior stair.

The second major factor affecting cost is the amount of work you do
yourself. You pay for materials and labor in a remodeling project. The
more labor you provide yourself, the lower the cost. Labor in this case
does not mean just driving nails or careful carpentry. It also means
supervision of subcontractors.

The most expensive way is to do none of the work yourself and to
hire a general contractor to oversee the subcontractors. According to one
study, you can save roughly 20 percent of that cost if you act as the
general contractor overseeing the subcontractors. Then you can save 20
percent more, or 40 percent total, if you are skilled enough to do quite
a bit of the work yourself. For readers who are unfamiliar with construction, it is important to remember that being a general contractor has its
own special set of skills. Not everybody will enjoy learning them on the
job, particularly when it is their own job they will be learning on. Chapter
7 discusses the do-it-yourself approach in more detail. For some, it may
be more expensive to do it yourself.

Regardless of what the cost is, it is important to have a good estimate
beforehand. This chapter will help you make a ballpark estimate. A
ballpark figure cannot replace a set of estimates by contractors, but it will
aid you in deciding whether or not it is worthwhile to install an accessory
apartment in your home. The first section of this chapter explains how
to estimate costs by the square-foot method; the second section explains
how to estimate costs by estimating the cost of each of the remodeling
tasks to be accomplished.

The Square-Foot Method

The square-foot method is a quick and simple way to estimate the cost
of your accessory apartment. All you need to know are the type of conversion you are doing (attic, basement, etc.), the amount of involvement
you will have in the remodeling work, and the relative quality of materials
you expect to use. With that in mind, review Table 6-1. This table uses
the name "secondary unit" for accessory apartments. It lists a square-foot
cost based on the above three factors. Once you've found the square-foot
cost that applies to you, multiply it by the number of square feet your
apartment will have, and you will have your estimate. A typical apartment

Table 6-1
Square-Foot Method of Cost Estimation*

Secondary Unit Type†	No Owner Involvement		Owner as General Contractor		Owner as General Contractor and Remodeler (Experienced)	
	High Quality ($/sq.ft.)	Standard Quality ($/sq.ft.)	High Quality ($/sq.ft.)	Standard Quality ($/sq.ft.)	High Quality ($/sq.ft.)	Standard Quality ($/sq.ft.)
Detached cottage‡ (stick-built)	65	52	52	42	39	32
Major addition	65	52	52	42	39	32
Internal conversion + small addition	50	40	40	32	30	24
Basement conversion	40	32	32	26	24	19
Garage conversion	50	40	40	32	30	24
Second-story addition	65	52	52	42	39	32
Second-story conversion	35	28	28	22	21	17
Attic conversion	65	52	52	42	39	32

*Figures represent median costs for the Bay Area. Conversion costs in specific instances will depend somewhat upon other factors.

†Note: Only these eight major conversion configurations were analyzed. Other, less common secondary-unit types include: conversion of detached garage, addition of second story over garage (attached or detached), and conversion of split-level dwelling.

‡Note: Several housing manufacturers in California offer factory-built modular cottages for $45–$55 per square foot, installed.

Source: *Second Units: An Emerging Housing Resource*, People for Open Space, San Francisco, California, June 1983.

is 500 to 700 square feet. To get the size of yours, measure each of the rooms or all of the space you are going to include in the apartment.

This table was prepared by People for Open Space in 1983. You might want to add to their figures to adjust for inflation since 1983. In addition, you may want to deflate their figures by 20 percent because San Francisco is a high-cost area for construction.

People for Open Space is a San Francisco environmental group that is interested in accessory apartments because they provide additional housing without requiring the development of additional raw land for housing sites.

The Task-by-Task Method

The task-by-task method will give you a more precise estimate of the cost of installing your apartment than the square-foot method, because you will be detailing the cost of each remodeling task. This method is not unlike what a contractor would do in coming to your home and preparing an estimate. In fact, the figures listed here come from the R. S. Means Company's *Repair and Remodeling Cost Data 1985*, which is a guidebook for contractors making estimates. The rough estimate you can develop from this chapter, however, cannot replace the estimation done by a professional contractor. (The cost information is copyrighted by R. S. Means Company, Inc., Kingston, Massachusetts. It is reproduced from *Repair and Remodeling Cost Data 1985* with permission.)

In deriving these tables from R. S. Means's *Repair and Remodeling Estimator*, we have simplified their presentation. Means gives costs in two ways: "unit price" and "systems." Systems costs for materials and labor include subcontractor overhead and profit. Unit price costs do not. We have drawn from both unit price costs and systems costs. Where unit price costs are the source, 10 percent has been added to the cost of materials to be consistent with systems costs, which include 10 percent subcontractor markup for "handling." Similarly, 53.8 percent for subcontractor overhead and profit has been added to labor costs from the unit price section to make them consistent with labor costs from the systems section. Finally, costs for special equipment needed for a few jobs have been included as part of the labor costs. These occur only infrequently and do not justify carrying a separate column throughout the tables.

It should also be noted that where Means gives a maximum and a minimum cost for an item (for example, a stove), the minimum price was taken. This was done because it was assumed that most apartments would be installed as inexpensively as possible.

Repair and Remodeling Cost Data would serve you well as a reference on costs and materials, especially if you are going to be your own general contractor. Its detailed information on costs of materials and labor is arranged in easily read tables, often supplemented with drawings. Information on how to obtain it is contained in Chapter 7, which covers installing the apartment yourself.

You should prepare yourself to read the rest of this section by getting together a calculator, a pencil, and paper, preferably graph paper or ledger paper. You should also have a preliminary plan for your apartment, or at least an idea of what it will look like. Write the following column headings on the paper:

Item	*Quantity*	*Materials*	*Labor*	*Total*

As you go through each section, write down the tasks you must complete to install your apartment. Not every task mentioned here will be precisely applicable to your situation. You may also need to adjust the volume of materials required. In some cases you may need to add tasks that are not covered here. In particular, you may also want to consider getting other work done on your home while the accessory apartment is being installed.

Before we go on, you should know what these cost figures include and exclude. First, the costs listed are for an inexpensive conversion, but they are not squeezed down to the bare minimum, and therefore they should adequately cover costs. You should feel free to explore cost-cutting alternatives. Second, the costs are those charged by subcontractors, so they include overhead and profit for the subcontractors but not for the general contractor. If you expect to work through a general contractor who in turn will hire and organize the subcontractors, add 20 percent to your total cost. R. S. Means suggests that in some cases the general contractor's costs will be less. However, from a contractor's perspective, accessory apartments are likely to be relatively small jobs that nonetheless involve a large amount of troubleshooting and consulting with owners, so 20 percent is probably a reasonable figure. Third, if you intend to do the work on a given task yourself, include only the cost of materials and not labor. You should remember, however, that even though the materials costs given include a 10 percent markup for the subcontractor, prices for materials to people in the building trade are often 20 percent less than they are to the homeowner. You should mark up the materials another 10 percent if you are using the figures to estimate materials only. Fourth, costs will vary by location. In *Repair and Remodeling Cost Data 1985,* construction price indexes are given for numerous cities, with 100 as the base average. The city with the highest construction costs is Anchorage, Alaska, at 134; the city with the lowest costs is Greensboro, North Carolina, at 82. Costs vary between large and small cities and between different areas of the United States. Look at the following cities as examples:

CALIFORNIA	San Francisco	123
	Anaheim	112
TEXAS	Houston	96
	El Paso	85
ILLINOIS	Chicago	99
	Springfield	98
NEW YORK	New York	112
	Binghamton	91

Now you can begin estimating the costs of individual tasks, from adding a bathroom to installing a utility meter. In some cases there may be items that you want to include that are not listed. For example, we were unable to come up with a good, usable way to estimate the cost of window wells for basements. Also, you may want a particular type of appliance—for example, a gas range instead of an electric one. A handy source of information for costs on a variety of appliances is a catalog from Sears or some other major mail-order company.

There is one final point you should know about the figures given here. It should also simplify your own calculations. The figures have been rounded to the nearest $5 except in the case of unit costs, which have been rounded to the nearest 5 cents. The purpose of rounding is to simplify calculations, and any error introduced will be insignificant in comparison to the error inherent in any estimate of this kind—and also in comparison to the time you will save.

Adding a Bathroom

If you don't need to add a bathroom, skip this section. If you do, here is a list of the individual costs of a three-fixture bathroom (Table 6-2).

The list includes fixtures such as a toilet, tub, and lavatory. It also includes accessories, such as lighting and floor treatment. Many homeowners will already have half-baths, which require only the addition of a tub and some partition changes. Some readers may not be familiar with two terms. "Water closet" means a toilet, and "rough-in" refers to the installation of the pipes necessary to serve a plumbing fixture.

Table 6-2
Adding a Bathroom

Item	Quantity	Materials	Labor	Total
Water closet, floor mounted, two-piece	1	$115	$ 90	$ 205
Rough-in for water closet	1	95	255	350
Bathtub, 5' cast iron w/ accessories	1	270	110	380
Rough-in for bathtub	1	90	390	480
Lavatory, 20" × 18" cast iron w/ accessories	1	125	60	185
Rough-in for lavatory	1	120	355	475
Toilet tissue dispenser, chrome, single roll	1	20	10	30
Towel Bar, 18" long, stainless steel	2	40	20	60
Medicine cabinet w/ mirror, 16" × 2" unlighted	1	45	15	60
Incandescent light, square glass lens w/ metal trim, prewired	1	20	40	60
Vinyl composition tile, 12" × 12", 1/16" thick	20 sq. ft.	10	10	20
Total		**$950**	**$1,355**	**$2,305**

Adding a Kitchen

Kitchens are typically the most expensive improvements made. This estimate includes plumbing, a sink, wall and base cabinets, a countertop, appliances, lighting, and floor treatment (Table 6-3).

Table 6-3
Adding a Kitchen

Item	Quantity	Materials	Labor	Total
Prefinished wood cabinets, average quality, wall and base	10 lin. ft.	$ 960	$140	$1,100
Custom laminated plastic countertop	10 lin. ft.	60	80	140
Stainless steel sink, 22″ × 25″	1	240	150	390
Faucet, top mount	1	30	25	55
Plumbing rough-in for sink	1	95	405	500
Range hood, 30″ two-speed, vented	1	65	45	110
Cooking range, 30″ free-standing, one oven	1	350	25	375
Refrigerator, no frost, 10–12 cu. ft.	1	385	40	425
Fluorescent strip lighting fixture, two lamps, mounting hardware, connections	1	20	35	55
Vinyl composition tile, 12″ × 12″, 1/16″ thick	70 sq. ft.	40	30	70
Total		**$2,245**	**$975**	**$3,220**

Adding an Entrance

Some homeowners may not need to add an entrance. Among those who do, the cost of the installation will vary considerably. Table 6-4 provides some examples.

Table 6-4
Adding an Entrance

Item	Quantity	Materials	Labor	Total
Adding a sidewalk to the entrance door:				
Asphalt sidewalk (bituminous), 2″ thick with gravel base	25 sq. yd.	$90	$360	$450

Item	Quantity	Materials	Labor	Total
Adding an exterior door:				
Cut door opening in wall			50	50
Frame, incl. exterior trim,				
5/4 × 5 $^3/_{16}$″ deep	17 lin. ft.	45	30	75
Steel door, 24 gauge, embossed, full panel, 3′ × 7′	1	140	30	170
Lockset	1	15	25	40
Weather stripping	1	10	30	40
Total		**$210**	**$165**	**$375**

Adding or Rebuilding a Staircase

Some homeowners may need to build or rebuild staircases. This is a difficult task to estimate without knowing the specific situation. Let's start with a set of concrete basement entrance stairs (Table 6-5).

Consider these costs from actual work done by the Minnesota Housing Finance Agency. These figures were developed specifically to address some of the problems unique to the installation of accessory apartments. (Ten percent has been added to their costs since the work was done in 1982.)

Table 6-5
Adding or Rebuilding a Staircase

Item	Quantity	Materials	Labor	Total
Basement entrance stairs 3′ wide	1 set	$420	$ 55	$ 475
Rebuild stairwells to change direction and make separate entrance to attic apartment	1 set	880	3,520	4,400
Enclose stairwell in two-story house to allow separate entrance to second-floor apartment	1 set	495	2,110	2,605

Adding a Parking Space

The local zoning regulations will probably require that you provide off-street parking for your tenant. Table 6-6 provides an estimate for a low-cost driveway. You should note that some jurisdictions have code requirements that affect the way driveways are built.

Table 6-6
Adding a Parking Space

Item	Quantity	Materials	Labor	Total
Asphalt driveway, 10' × 30' w/ 2" binder, 1" topping on 6" crushed stone, sealed	1	$280	$305	$585

Adding Heating and Air Conditioning

In most cases the simplest way to add heating and air conditioning is to use self-contained electrical units. You might want also to consider adding new ducts onto your existing system. Think about the advantage of having "zoned" controls. Typically, homes are controlled by one thermostat, which could mean that you and your tenant would have to agree on how warm or cool the home should be. If you are going to add on to your existing system, you may want to see if separate controls can be installed. Separate controls may be required by some local governments.

One of the advantages of self-contained electrical units is that they provide zone control as a matter of course. Tables 6-7 and 6-8 offer some estimates for them. Additions to existing heating and cooling systems will have to be developed individually by contractors or subcontractors.

Table 6-7
Adding Heat

Item	Quantity	Materials	Labor	Total
Electric baseboard heater, 4' long	3	$140	$120	$260
Thermostat, integral	1	15	15	30
12-3 copper wire w/ ground	80 lin. ft.	20	100	120
Panel board breaker, 20 amp	1	15	35	50
Outlet box	3	5	45	50
Total		**$195**	**$315**	**$510**

Table 6-8
Adding Air Conditioning

Item	Quantity	Materials	Labor	Total
Window-unit air conditioner, semipermanent installation, three-speed fan, high-efficiency, 10,000 BTUH, four-way, high-thrust	1	$485	$40	$525
Air conditioning receptacle	1	5	30	35
Total		$490	$70	$560

Separating Utility Meters

If you decide you want the electrical utility meter of your tenant to be separate from your own, estimate the following cost for a single-phase 100-amp service, the typical electrical installation to serve a house (Table 6-9).

Table 6-9
Separating Utility Meters

Item	Quantity	Materials	Labor	Total
Weathercap	1	$ 5	$ 20	$ 25
Service entrance cable	20 lin. ft.	15	50	65
Meter socket	1	20	80	100
Entrance disconnect switch	1	110	140	250
Ground rod, with clamp	1	15	50	65
Ground cable	10 lin. ft.	10	15	25
Panel board, 12 circuit	1	95	220	315
Total		$270	$575	$845

Few homeowners install separate water meters voluntarily, since the cost of water is low. The savings from being able to bill tenants separately for water is not enough to justify the expense of installing separate water service in most cases.

Adding Electrical Outlets

In parts of the apartment you may need to add electrical outlets, switches, or lighting wires. The estimate in Table 6-10 will give you the unit cost of each wiring type. Multiply that cost by the number of units you need to add for your apartment.

Table 6-10
Adding Electrical Outlets

Item	Quantity	Materials	Labor	Total
Outlet (duplex receptacle), nonmetallic sheathed cable	1	$5	$20	$25
Switch, single pole, nonmetallic sheathed cable	1	5	15	20
Lighting wiring, nonmetallic sheathed cable	per light	5	15	20
Lighting fixture, 150 watt, incandescent, recess mounted, prewired	1	40	35	75

Adding and Removing Walls

The interior wall estimate is given in two parts: first, the cost per square foot, and second, the total cost for an average-sized (8-foot-high by 9-foot-long) wall. With the unit cost figure you can estimate for the size of your own wall(s), while the 8-foot-by-9-foot wall figure offers a general estimate (Table 6-11). If you are furring an exterior wall—preparing the interior side with wood studs and dry wall—use one-half the cost per square foot.

Table 6-11
Adding and Removing Walls

Item	Quantity	Materials	Labor	Total
Unit costs				
Wood studs, 2" × 4", 16" on center, 8' high	0.125 sq. ft.	$ .35	$ .65	$1.00

Item	Quantity	Materials	Labor	Total
Gypsum drywall, ⅝" thick	2 sq. ft.	.50	.55	1.05
Taping and finishing	2 sq. ft.	.05	.50	.55
Insulation, 3½" fiberglass batts	1 sq. ft.	.20	.15	.35
Baseboard, painted	0.2 lin. ft.	.15	.40	.55
Painting, roller, two coats	2 sq. ft.	.20	.50	.70
Total unit cost	1 sq. ft.	$1.45	$2.75	$4.20
Total wall cost 8' × 9'	72 sq. ft.	**$105.00**	**$200.00**	**$305.00**

If you are removing a wall, estimate the minimum charge per square foot at $0.38 for studs and drywall and $0.67 for studs and plaster. If there is wiring or plumbing in the wall that has to be moved, that will add to the cost and these estimates will be low.

Painting the Walls

Finally, you will want to paint the apartment (Table 6-12).

Table 6-12
Painting the Walls

Item	Quantity	Materials	Labor	Total
Painting on plaster or drywall: roller work, primer and one coat	sq. ft.	.05	.20	.25
600 sq. ft. apartment, with 3 rooms, each 10' × 20' × 8' plus ceilings = 2,040 sq. ft.	2,040 sq. ft.	100	410	510

Adding a Ceiling

A typical ceiling will be gypsum drywall. Table 6-13 provides a square-foot cost estimate for a ceiling as well as a total cost for a 500-square-foot ceiling. Insulation will probably be needed only for attics and garages. In many cases a new ceiling will not be needed.

Table 6-13
Adding a Ceiling

Item	Quantity	Materials	Labor	Total
Unit costs				
Gypsum drywall, 4′ × 8′, ⁵/₈″ thick, screwed	1 sq. ft.	$ .25	$ .40	$ .65
Main runners, 1¹/₂″ cold-rolled channel, 4′ on center	0.5 sq. ft.	.10	.30	.40
25 ga. channels, 2′ on center	1 sq. ft.	.20	.50	.70
Taping and finishing	1 sq. ft.	.00	.25	.25
Painting, two coats roller work	1 sq. ft.	.10	.25	.35
Total unit cost	1 sq. ft.	.65	1.70	2.35
Total ceiling cost	500 sq. ft.	$325.00	$850.00	$1,175.00

Looking at the Total Cost

If you go back and add up the costs for the individual tasks needed for your apartment from the figures above, you should have an estimate of the total cost (Table 6-14). Remember, however, that it is a rough estimate, and be sure to add 20 percent for the cost of a general contractor.

Table 6-14
Total Cost of the Accessory Apartment

Bath	$2,305
Kitchen	3,220
Entrance	
sidewalk	450
exterior door	375
stairway	2,605
parking	585
Heating	510
Air conditioning	560
Outlets (4)	100

Switches (3)	60
Lighting fixtures (3) and wiring	285
Wall (8' × 9')	305
Remove plaster wall, 8' × 10'	55
Painting	510
Ceiling (500 sq. ft.)	1,175
Subtotal	13,100
General contractor @ 20%	2,620
Total	**$15,720**

The total cost of the accessory apartment for which we have prepared an estimate will be about $15,700. Yours may vary considerably from that figure. Regardless of the amount, having an estimate in which you have at least a little confidence gives you one of the building blocks for making a decision about whether or not it makes financial sense to go ahead and install an accessory apartment.

Financing Your Accessory Apartment

The next thing to think about is how you are going to pay for the installation. Many people will be able to choose how to pay for the installation of the accessory apartment. Typically, the choice will be between paying for it out of savings or getting a loan to pay for it. The advantage of using your savings is that you will have no extra costs for interest. The advantage of getting a loan, even if you have savings, is that if you need the savings for other opportunities, or for an emergency, you will still have them available for use.

Paying as You Go

Another option is to pay for the remodeling on an incremental basis. If the installation cost is moderate and you are doing most of the work yourself, this is probably a good option. The drawback is that the completion of the project is spread over the period of months when you are earning the money and doing the work, so your household might be in the midst of a construction project for an intolerable period. In addition, you may have to schedule carefully so that you can afford materials when you are ready to install them.

Borrowing from Family or Friends

If your personal resources can't finance the remodeling project, you must borrow the money. There might be a friend or relative who would be willing to lend you money. Such loans can draw people closer together, but they can also sour relationships forever. The only rule that seems to be generally true is the line of poetry by Robert Frost: "Good fences make good neighbors." If you are going to take a loan from a friend or a relative, make sure the terms of the loan are clear, and insist on a written contract. Though the matter may appear simple and easily agreed upon at the onset, circumstances may change with time. Conflicts over use of the money and repayment could surface in later months. If you can rely on the written agreement instead of your remembrance of a verbal agreement, any conflict will be more easily settled. Specify in your contract such things as the interest rate, the monthly payment, what happens when a payment is late, what happens if you can't repay the loan, and whether or not there is any penalty for early repayment.

For many homeowners, the best route will be to borrow the money from a bank, savings and loan institution, or mortgage finance company. The major questions will be whether or not you can convince lenders of your ability to repay the loan and, if you can, what interest rate they will charge you.

The following sections describe, in more detail than you may want to read, most of the possible steps you can take to obtain a loan. If you take them as an exhaustive checklist, every one of which has to be pursued in detail before you make a decision, you yourself will probably be exhausted before you obtain a loan. Instead, use them as a review of the possibilities, just as you would look for the best way to take a step over a puddle without breaking your stride.

Shopping for the Best Loan

To find the right loan, you will need to shop around. Just as it takes time and effort to find the new car best suited to your needs at the lowest price, it takes time and effort to find the loan best suited to your circumstances at the lowest interest rate. In your shopping, you will have to compare interest rates, loan types, and lending institutions. However, as noted above, don't feel you have to be exhaustive about it.

Interest Rates

Banks seek low-risk borrowers, and they have a showroom of loan options. The two basic options are fixed and variable interest rates. The fixed rate, a long-held tradition, has a set rate for the duration of the loan period. In contrast, the variable rate, a new loan innovation, has a rate that fluctuates with the supply of money available to lend. The fixed rate offers you a secure rate of interest. The variable rate offers you a lower interest rate to begin with, but at the risk that it may move up and down according to money-market conditions.

A fixed interest rate is generally the best choice. But if only a variable loan is available, or it is offered at a rate substantially below the fixed rate, be sure that an interest rate cap is a part of the loan. The cap sets a limit as to how high the interest rate may rise.

Types of Loans

Another important characteristic of loans is the collateral required as security for the loan. Since you are a homeowner, you will most likely use the equity in your home as collateral, but take a moment to look at all the different types of loans available. Remember, too, that financial institutions create new loan types as the competition demands.

Home Improvement Loans.   A home improvement loan may be secured or unsecured. The unsecured loan will generally be at a higher interest rate. Typically, however, the equity you have in your home—that is, how much of it you own above and beyond any outstanding mortgage—will be the security of the loan. In addition to this security, with a home-improvement loan the lender may require that you state the intended use of the money. You may even be required to show proof of how the money was used as the installation of the accessory apartment progresses. Home improvement loans typically have fixed interest rates. They also have closing costs.

Second Mortgages.   A second mortgage loan is also secured by the equity you have in your home. The second mortgage is like a first mortgage, the difference being that the first mortgage has first claim of repayment in the event that the borrower defaults on the loan. The risk to the lender is therefore higher than on a first mortgage, and so the interest rate is often higher. However, since interest rates vary with current money market conditions, your second mortgage rate could be either higher or lower than your first. If you got your first mortgage a good many years ago, the second mortgage interest rate will almost certainly be higher. The interest rate on a second mortgage is generally fixed, and there will be closing costs associated with it.

Refinanced Mortgages.   You may find that your best source of financing is to refinance your present mortgage. This is especially apt to be true if interest rates have fallen below the rate at which you purchased your home. In this case you will have only one mortgage, which will now include the cost of remodeling as well as the money you still have to repay on your original mortgage. If you consider this possibility, be wary of variable-rate mortgages. With a variable rate mortgage there's a risk that you will end up paying more interest on the loan in the future. You will also pay closing costs.

Home Equity Line of Credit.   Lines of credit, similar to credit card accounts but for larger amounts, are a new innovation of banks. They, too, are secured by the equity in your home. You can automatically borrow up to a set limit for any purpose, without any questions. The advantage is that you don't have to ask repeatedly for loans to be approved, but instead have a continuous source of loans. There are, however, two possible disadvantages of using home equity lines of credit to install accessory apartments. First, the interest rates may be higher than for other types of loans. Second, the interest rates may be variable.

HUD Insured Loans.   The U.S. Department of Housing and Urban Development (HUD) insures loans for home improvement. The loans they insure are offered through private financial institutions—banks and savings and loans—and are called FHA Title I loans. FHA stands for Federal Housing Administration and Title I refers to the relevant section of the National Housing Act. The purpose of HUD's involvement is to help people get credit by insuring loans. The insurance reduces the lender's risk and therefore increases the lender's eagerness to loan money.

A Title I(b) loan is set up to finance the conversion of an existing structure to one that will house two families: your single-family home converted to include an accessory apartment. The maximum term of the loan is 15 years, and the rate is the current daily rate offered by the bank. The maximum amount you can borrow is $8,750 per dwelling unit. So, for your two units, you can borrow up to $17,500. Also note that there is no prepayment penalty.

HUD Title 1(b) loans are also offered through contractors approved by lenders that offer the loans. The contractors are approved by the lending institution and not by HUD. The contractor acts as an intermediary between you and the bank. Loans issued through the contractor will typically be 1 to 2 percentage points above the rate of a loan you obtain for yourself from a lender. The contractor's five-step procedure for arranging this type of loan is outlined in Appendix 9. The easiest way to find a participating contractor or bank is to call your local bank. There are 4,000 banks in the program nationwide.

Life Insurance Loans.   Life insurance companies allow you to borrow the current cash value of your life insurance, since it is your money and they are just holding on to it for you. These are typically low-interest, fixed-rate loans. The risk here is undercutting the value of your life insurance while the loan is outstanding.

Loans for People with Low Incomes.   Local housing commissions often loan money at low interest rates to provide housing for lower income persons. If you are at a low income level, or are willing to house a lower-income person in your accessory apartment, you may qualify for one of these loans.

Personal Loans.   Another option is personal loans. These can be secured or unsecured, depending on the size of the loan and/or the choice of the borrower, and the rates vary according to whether the loan is secured or not. The rate might be fixed or variable. Personal loans offered through finance companies tend to have high interest rates.

Types of Lending Institutions

Loans are available through a variety of lending institutions: commercial banks, savings and loan institutions, credit unions, finance companies, and life insurance companies. Each of them is reviewed below to give you a feeling for whether it would be the right place for you to try to get a loan for an accessory apartment.

Commercial Banks.   Commercial banks offer personal loans, home-improvement loans, home-equity loans, second mortgages, mortgage refinancing, and HUD Title I loans. The interest rates are average for the loan types, with some institutions having higher rates and some lower ones. Your chances for getting a loan are better if you currently have an account with the bank.

Savings and Loan Institutions.   Savings and loans offer home-improvement loans, home-equity loans, second mortgages, mortgage refinancing, and HUD Title I loans. Savings and loans are more active in home remodeling loans than are commercial banks. If you have a savings account or your first mortgage with a savings and loan, it is more likely to give you a loan for an accessory apartment. The rates at a savings and loan are usually about the same as those at a commercial bank.

Credit Unions.   Credit unions offer personal and home-improvement loans. You will be able to get a loan only if you are a member. Credit unions have limits on the amount members can borrow, so you may run into problems if you need a large loan for your apartment. Interest rates are usually lower than those of commercial banks.

Finance Companies.   Finance companies offer personal and home-improvement loans. The loans are quite easy to get, but you will often pay higher interest rates.

Life Insurance Companies.   Since life insurance companies offer loans on insurance policies, you obviously need to have a policy with the company. This source will probably offer the lowest possible interest rate. The problem, as noted earlier, is that borrowing against your life insurance reduces its payoff by an equivalent amount in the event of your death.

Asking for the Loan

After you have done some investigative window shopping, you are ready to go out and ask about loans. What you must prove is simple: that you will repay the loan. The lender will go through a checklist of items to analyze you as a credit risk.

Keep in mind your rights under the Truth in Lending law, which basically provides that, in the maze of loan costs, percentages, points, etc., you can require that the institution quote to you the total cost of the loan. This, like the unit price labels in the grocery store, should allow you to compare the interest rates of the loans you are offered.

Your Credit Check

The lender will check your credit by comparing your assets and your liabilities. In other words, he or she will look at whether your cash savings, securities, and properties outweigh your debts, bills due, and unpaid taxes. The lender will also check your income and employment stability to determine your ability to repay the loan. Finally, the lender will check into your credit history to determine whether you have a good reputation for making loan payments. He or she will call up a credit reporting agency to get information on your credit accounts; loan accounts; records of bankruptcy, tax liens, or judgments; bills turned over to a collection agency; and your previous addresses and employers.

Proof of Rental Income

You are probably planning to use the income you receive in rent to pay off the remodeling loan. However, be aware that some lenders will frown upon the idea. They tend to want a signed lease to prove to them that you will be getting income from the accessory apartment. This may be difficult if the apartment does not yet exist.

If you have adequate income to pay off the loan without any reliance on the rental income, you have no problem. But if the rental income is critical to proving you can pay back the loan, the lender may deny your application. Accessory apartments are new things to most lenders. Most loan officers are encouraged to go by the book in estimating risks, and accessory apartments are often not even in their book. Still, if you have a good credit rating, and can describe past loans and mortgages you have had and repaid, you may carry the day.

Lenders' Reactions to Single-Family-Home Conversions

The conversion of single-family homes is a new idea to many lenders. Many accept it as an innovation that stimulates their own lending avenues; others shy from its nonconventionality. Some lenders haven't even known that they were financing an accessory apartment. If you get a home-improvement loan or a second mortgage, it is likely the bank will know what you are doing with the money. It is sure to know if you cite the rental income from the apartment as the source of income from which you will repay the loan. Be aware that lenders react differently to the idea and that you might have to do a sales pitch for accessory apartments while asking for the loan. Lenders will tend to react particularly badly if you ask for a loan to install an apartment before the local government has made them legal. What the lender will want to know more than anything else is that the apartment will make money for you, because then you will be able to repay the loan. To convince him or her that it will make money, prepare for your own case the financial analysis we go through later on in this chapter, in the section titled "Is It Worth It?"

Requirements for Blueprints and Estimates

Typically you will not be required to verify your use of the loan money to the lending institution, but there are two exceptions. The first is a home improvement loan in which you have limited equity in the home. Because it is a loan of greater risk, the bank wants to make sure its money goes back into the item of collateral. Therefore, the lender may want to see blueprints and contractor estimates. The second instance is a HUD Title I loan. In this case you will have to develop with the contractor a detailed statement of the work to be done.

If the Answer Is No

If you are denied a loan, do not give up. Your first step is to find out exactly what kept you from getting the loan. You might need simply to give further proof of your credit history or ability to repay the loan. If it looks hopeless at that institution, think about whether the same problem would come up at a different financial institution.

Estimating Rental Income

The easiest way to find out what you could rent your apartment for is to look at what apartments rent for in the neighborhoods nearby. If you look in the apartment listings in your local paper, you should be able to get a sense pretty rapidly. Look for apartments that are the same size that yours will be. If your apartment will offer special features, such as a fireplace, or some private yard space of its own, then you can move the rent up a little. If there are drawbacks to it, such as no view except the neighbor's aluminum siding, or a very small kitchen, then the rent you charge should be lower. Another way is to call local real estate agents who manage rental property. They are generally willing to share a little of their knowledge in the hope that getting known will eventually result in people selling homes through them. Finally, you can call the local housing agency and find out what the vacancy rate for rental apartments is. In tight markets, where the vacancy rate is low and there are few apartments to rent, the trend in rental rates is generally up. If this is the case in your area, then you can have more confidence in the ability of your apartment to pull in a good rental income. The vacancy rate is also a good indicator of how long it will take you to find a good tenant.

An important point to remember when thinking about your rental income is that the apartment may sometimes be vacant between tenants. Owners of apartment buildings often assume that a typical apartment will be vacant 10 percent of the time when trying to estimate whether or not a building is a financially sound investment. For our purposes here let us assume that yours will be vacant one month out of the year. In practice, your apartment may almost never be vacant, but this conservative assumption may protect you from making a bad investment in an accessory apartment. If an occasional month without rental income would be intolerable for you, an accessory apartment may be too much of a gamble.

Another factor to take into account when thinking about the rent you will charge is who will be paying utilities. In most cases it will be you, because of the added cost of providing separate meters for the apartment. You should estimate how much the tenant will add to your utility bills and include that with the rent. If you are not sure, make an estimate that protects you. You can always lower the rent if you think you have overcharged the tenant by $10 or $15 per month. Raising it unexpectedly, however, will probably be difficult and will certainly make your tenant unhappy.

Will you be asking for any services from your tenant as part of the rent? If so, the rent should be reduced accordingly. Service exchanges are discussed in more detail in Chapter 9, and you may want to refer to it now. However, the important issue for this discussion is that you cannot expect services without offering adequate compensation, and without restricting the number of people interested in your apartment.

Is It Worth It?

The simplest way to look at an accessory apartment is to see whether or not it is going to make money for you. You may be installing it for other reasons—for added security, perhaps, or to get services, or to be sure there is someone in the house while you spend the winters in Florida. Even so, looking at its profit potential is a good place to start. Then you can add in the value you place on its other benefits, and subtract any value you place on its costs, such as the time it may take you to manage it.

Table 6-15 is based on the example of an empty nester couple on the East Coast. They have decided not only that they are tired of living alone, but also that they want some extra income so they can take some trips to California to see their grandchildren, and maybe even stop in Las Vegas on the way.

In any case, they own a home that originally cost $60,000 and was bought before 1981. The value of the lot at the time of purchase was $12,000. A third of the house will be used for the apartment. This set of facts, when combined with utility rates and other necessary assumptions about repairs, yields the figures in the table. Details for the table are in Appendix II.

In the example given above, the homeowner makes a nice profit. That may not always be the case. Suppose the apartment was much more expensive. Suppose it cost about $30,000 to install because it was in a basement that required excavation and new windows in order to get good light and ventilation. This would add about $1,800 to costs after deduc-

Table 6-15
Net Change in Annual Income from an Accessory Apartment

Rental income ($436/month × 11 months; assumes 1 month vacancy)	$4,800
Tax deductions from accessory apartment	889
Payments on loan to install apartment ($16,000 over 10 years @ 15%)	−1,936
Total income from accessory apartment after expenses and taxes	**$3,753**

tions. As a result, the profitability of the apartment would drop dramatically, to about $1,700 per year. From the point of view of many homeowners, particularly those who do not look forward to the idea of managing a tenant, the profit might not be great enough for the time and risks involved.

On the other hand, assume the $30,000 cost in the case of a single parent who might want the added security of having someone next door, and the opportunity to get some services such as occasional babysitting. Assume the babysitting is once a week at $10 per time. Profit would be further reduced by $480 per year to about $1,200, but it might still be worthwhile installing the apartment for the services and the security in addition to the income.

The same kind of choice often results in the installation of accessory apartments essentially without any financial analysis. One couple in their fifties installed an accessory apartment in their home for the husband's mother, even though it was clearly too expensive an installation ever to make renting the unit profitable. However, it is always good to do the financial analysis. Most accessory apartments are not used exclusively for either family or strangers. In practice they tend to move between the two types of uses over time. The financial analysis will give homeowners considering the installation of an apartment for an older relative or a recently married child a great deal more confidence about what they are doing. It may also help them decide whether or not added expenses, such as a dishwasher or a private patio, will be worthwhile investments in the long run.

To help you run your own financial analysis, we have included as Appendix 10 a detailed pro forma, with footnotes. You can use it as a model. Note, however, that if you bought or will buy your home after 1981, you have to use the ACRS method of depreciation.

It is also worthwhile to look, not just at the cost and profit of the accessory apartment, but also at the costs of alternative ways to achieve the same objective.

In the case of the couple mentioned above who installed an accessory apartment for the husband's mother, the alternative was to pay rental for service-enriched housing or a group home which included services. In the case of the group home with services, the cost would have been a little over $12,000 per year. Although that figure included some medical services, it still seemed too expensive, particularly since the mother would have gone through her personal capital in three or four years. Instead, she invested in the accessory apartment along with her son and daughter-in-law, and they protected both her personal independence and some of her financial security.

On the other hand, installing the accessory apartment may not always be the answer. If security is simply the most important issue, and you do not mind giving up some of your privacy, it may be much cheaper simply to take a tenant in your home as it now exists. Shared housing, or "taking a roomer," as it used to be called, requires no capital investment. The income can be as great as or greater than the income from an accessory apartment, depending on how much it costs to install one in your home.

In summary, the profit potential of an accessory apartment is not always the most critical issue. In some cases, the profit may indeed be the most important point, but in others, the apartment may offer benefits regardless of potential profit. In still others, there may be better ways to achieve your goals. It is important, then, to be as clear as possible about your own personal objectives in installing the apartment. Consider carefully all costs and benefits, material and otherwise, before you make your decision.

Finally, remember the discussion in Chapter 2 about the hidden costs of installing an accessory apartment. The process of installing the apartment has its own costs. There is a great deal to learn and a lot of time that must be invested in getting the apartment installed. These costs are hard to put a dollar figure on, but they should not be forgotten in deciding whether or not to install an apartment.

=========== CHAPTER 7 ===========

DOING IT YOURSELF AND GETTING PERMITS

This chapter is divided into two parts. The first part covers the risks of installing an accessory apartment yourself. It is a pessimistic presentation about doing it yourself. It can be skipped by two groups of readers: those who know a lot about remodeling and those who don't want to know a lot about remodeling. Its objective is to reduce the number of homeowners who end up surrounded by unfinished walls, unpaid bills, and unending dreams about how much easier it would have been to hire a contractor. The discussion emphasizes risks and carefully avoids any mention of either the personal satisfaction or the financial savings from doing some or all of the work yourself.

The second part of the chapter discusses the various permits that are needed to install an accessory apartment. It will be useful even to those who do not intend to do any work on their apartment themselves. It explains the hoops through which most local governments will make the homeowner jump in order to install an accessory apartment. If you hire a contractor, one benefit will be that the contractor will jump through the hoops for you. However, it will still be useful for you to know what hoops he or she is jumping through on your behalf.

All or Part

The Learning Costs

People come to home remodeling with different abilities. You might be a person who enjoys working with your hands. Maybe you have a knack for carpentry or painting. If so, you may very well be eager to take on a remodeling job. On the other hand, you might be a person who shies away from doing things yourself. Maybe you became frustrated in the past when working on your home. Maybe the project took twice as long as you predicted or the quality of the finished product was below your expectations. If so, you will probably respond to the idea of doing it yourself with the same sinking feeling most people get when they realize they have locked their keys in their car.

Thinking about how well you can do remodeling tasks, as well as the time you have available to learn new skills, will help you decide how much of the remodeling to do yourself.

Have you ever seen a beautifully restored antique in a store that made you want to try refinishing a piece of your own furniture? Refinishing a piece of furniture often seems like a simple, straightforward job with exciting results. Then the excitement gets lost in endless sanding of intricate corners. The fumes of paint stripper that started out just tickling your nose end up irritating it. Finally, despite your high hopes and hard work, the piece comes out looking more thrift shop than antique. You start to strip the chair again in a fit of frustration, and finally you leave it to sit on a lonely patch of newspaper in the basement, looking like a scarred tank from some historic battle—only in this case, it's not a memorial with grass all around it. Every time you see it, the yellowing newspaper reminds you of how long the unfinished battle has been unfinished. You may finally regird your sandpaper, go back to work, and end up with a finished antique of your own, along with some skill at refinishing.

For the purposes of this discussion, the pertinent question is, How long did it take you? What probably took most of the time and caused most of the frustration was the cost of learning what you were doing. Or, the cost of learning you didn't know what you were doing.

Cabinetmakers have ways of refinishing furniture rapidly, but they often have special tools and almost always have been through a long apprenticeship. There is a learning cost involved in doing almost any home repair. The price of learning how to refinish furniture can be high.

The price of learning how to do home remodeling can be higher. Obviously, if you are already experienced in remodeling, there will be little or no learning cost involved. But novice do-it-yourselfers need to think about learning costs as they decide what work to involve themselves in.

Tasks with Very High Learning Costs

There are some tasks that you probably should not take on yourself unless you have had training. Examples are plumbing, electrical work, and, to a lesser extent, masonry. If mistakes are made in these areas, they can lead to serious problems over time. They can also lead to your having to put in overtime, to the need to rip out work that has already been done, and to increased expense. Imagine that you have put in all the wiring for your apartment and then the building inspector comes along and you find that you have not used the right wiring; you haven't got enough capacity for the bathroom heating unit. And, in addition, you find that you have located the wiring box for the bathroom light a little too low, and that it needs to be moved so that the medicine cabinet and mirror can fit in. Finally, you forgot that you were going to need 220-volt service for the electric stove. Imagine how much pleasure you would give some vindictive building inspector who has a chance to show how much he or she knows, and how little you do.

Another job that has a high learning cost is being your own general contractor. At least three skills are needed to be a general contractor. First, you need to know whether work has been done well or badly. Second, you need to be able to estimate accurately how long it will take to do a given job so that you are not paying a carpenter to wait for a plumber to finish up. Third, you will need to have the confidence to act at times like you know what you are doing when you don't, or in other words, to bluff. Some of these skills are hard to learn on your first job. In particular, it is hard for many people to learn how to ask innocent questions of subcontractors when they are simultaneously suspicious of the quality of the work that has been done and afraid of confronting the person who has done it.

Tasks with Moderate Learning Costs

There are some tasks which you could accomplish with moderate learning costs—that is, with a little experience and some tips from someone who has had a lot of experience. These tasks are called the finishing tasks:

rough carpentry, putting up wallboard, painting, and laying carpet. Often they are time-consuming and so carry with them high labor costs. Once you get the technique down, you can provide your own free labor and save substantial amounts of money.

It should be remembered, however, that these tasks still require careful work and plenty of time if the work is to be enjoyable and successful. If you aren't skilled, try not to undertake painting the day before a tenant is moving in, or framing in a wall the morning before the electrician is coming to mount a switch box in it. In general, never get caught doing a particular kind of work for the first time if someone else is depending on you to have it finished quickly.

Tasks with Few Learning Costs

Some tasks have few learning costs. They are tasks you can attack with confidence, and you can save money by doing them yourself. Examples are designing the apartment, which is discussed in Chapter 3, and decorating the apartment. Designing the apartment in detail will almost always be helpful, because in practice you will have to make most of the decisions about design yourself. An architect or contractor can work with you on a plan, but the decisions will be yours. In addition, the more work you put into the design at the beginning, the less likely it will be that you will want to go back during construction and make changes. Ideally, your plans should be made months ahead of the beginning of construction, so you can maximize use of labor time and avoid predictable problems. For example, it makes little sense to be deciding on what the entrance arrangement will be when the indoor stairways are being refinished, or to lay down new carpeting just before you paint.

For those seriously interested in do-it-yourself home building and remodeling who want to read further on the subject, we recommend the following two books:

Home Renovation
Francis D. K. Ching and Dale E. Miller
Van Nostrand Reinhold Co., Inc.
135 West 50th Street
New York, NY 10020
Cost: $15.95

This comprehensive guide for remodeling projects will be especially useful in planning the design of your apartment. The language can be easily understood by the layperson.

> *Repair and Remodeling Cost Data 1985* (updated annually)
> Robert Snow Means Company, Inc.
> 100 Construction Plaza
> P. O. Box 800
> Kingston, MA 02364-0800
> Cost: $37.95

The costs in Chapter 6 were derived from this cost-estimating guide for professional remodelers. Costs are given by building components (concrete, doors, pipes, etc.) and by systems (bathroom, kitchen, complete ceiling, etc.). The book's detail and step-by-step logic will be appreciated by do-it-yourselfers. It is expensive, and it could probably be used at a local library, but if you are going to be seriously involved in estimating the costs of your apartment, the book will probably be well worth its price to you. Remember that the prices in the book are prices to professionals, not individuals.

Building Codes and Permits

Building codes are designed to ensure that housing is built and maintained well enough to provide shelter and promote good health. To enforce these codes, local governments will monitor the remodeling of your home. They will do this through issuing permits and making home inspections. The methods change from one locality to the next, but the general purpose is the same. The guide to Montgomery County regulations at the end of Chapter 3 summarizes the requirements of several county agencies, without going into which agency was responsible for ensuring what.

Building Code Requirements

Building codes regulate the construction of a home so that it conforms to a minimum standard of construction quality. They cover such things as structural soundness and resistance to weather and fire. They control the design of floors, walls, roofs, structural beams, plumbing, and gas and electricity lines, as well as the materials that are used in all of these components. Building codes also require conformance to minimum standards for living space by regulating such things as room size, ceiling heights, ventilation, and light. These were covered in more detail in Chapter 3.

The remodeling work you do on your home must comply with the building code established for your community. So, as you plan your apartment you should refer to the building code to ensure that your design will be approved. Be aware that throughout the planning and construction phases you will have to show that your home is in compliance with the code. If you have a general contractor, he or she will get the relevant permits and schedule the requisite inspections. If you are doing it yourself, you will have to work directly with local government offices that regulate planning, building, health, fire, and water. Copies of the relevant sections of the codes, as well as explanations, are available from these offices.

Don't hesitate to ask local building inspectors for assistance. In Montgomery County, Maryland, the county government will send the building inspector out to talk to homeowners about the design of apartments even when they are just beginning to think about it. Also, as one contractor pointed out, many building inspectors are tired of spending their days bouncing back and forth between aggressive contractors and slimy slumlords. They will often be grateful for the opportunity to talk to an average citizen.

Permits You Will Need

Local governments control your compliance with building codes for new construction through permit issuance. The types of permits issued depend on the alterations you are planning to do: carpentry, electrical work, plumbing, or mechanical work. Each locality makes its own rules, so it is necessary for you to get information locally. However, the general types of permits will be mentioned here. Once again, the purpose of the permits is the same from location to location; only the processing details change.

The Zoning Permit.   As discussed in Chapter 4, zoning ordinances are local laws that regulate the way land can be used in any neighborhood. From the point of view of zoning officials in most communities, renting out a portion of your home changes the use. Assuming an ordinance permitting accessory apartments is in place, you will have to get a permit before you go ahead with your plans to install an apartment. In some localities, the permit process is relatively painless. But in others, where the politics of accessory apartments is sensitive, the process can be lengthy and complex. Chapter 4 discusses zoning related to accessory apartments and gives some advice on what to do if no ordinance is in place.

Typically, getting a zoning permit for an accessory apartment will require filing an application for a special exception. Special exceptions generally require hearings before a planning board or a board of appeals. Usually your neighbors will be notified and given a chance to comment on your application. The application will be reviewed to see that your lot complies with the size required by the zoning ordinance for accessory apartments and to see that other specific requirements are met, such as the size of your apartment; the availability of parking; and the prohibition against exterior modifications, such as separate entrances on the front of the house or exterior stairs.

The Building Permit.   As was mentioned earlier, you must apply for approval to change the structure of your home. The rule of thumb is that a permit is required for house alterations that go beyond general repairs. Sometimes a general permit is issued. Other times "subpermits" are issued to change different systems—plumbing, electrical, mechanical, or whatever.

To apply for a building permit, you must submit your remodeling plans to the local building department. These plans must be precise measurements of the structural changes. Some localities require that the plans be signed by an architect or engineer. You will also be assessed a fee, which is often based on the anticipated cost of construction. These plans must be reviewed by the zoning, building, sanitation, and health departments, and you should receive approval within a few weeks, often less. If the plans are not approved, the reasons why will be explained, and you will have to make alterations in your plans.

In Appendix 12 is an explanation of how to apply for a building permit for an accessory apartment or "ohana" unit. This explanation, prepared by the city and county of Honolulu, gives you a more detailed description of the information you or your architect or contractor must submit in order to get a building permit. Note that it also requires prechecks by various city departments to ensure that in principle everything is okay for you to proceed before you go to the actual work of preparing detailed submissions for the building permit. (See Appendix 11.)

The Occupancy Permit.   An occupancy permit is issued when all of the inspectors have approved the construction work. This permit has a very simple purpose: It gives official permission for the newly created or newly altered space to be occupied.

The Rental Permit or License.   In some areas you will be considered an official landlord in the community and therefore you will be required to have a permit or license to rent out your apartment. The housing or landlord tenant office is where you should inquire about the permit. You will be assessed a fee, approximately $20. Then an inspector will visit your home. The inspector will not be the same person as the building inspector, but he or she will probably accompany the building inspector who makes your final inspection. The rental permit will probably require renewal every year or two thereafter. A rental permit fee and inspection will be required at each renewal.

Building Inspectors

Building inspectors make site visits to ensure that the work is being done according to code. You will have at least one inspection for your remodeling job, and probably you will have several. Each alteration of a system—plumbing, mechanical, or electrical—may require an inspection. Often two are required—one when the system is roughed in and one when it is finished. An inspector will typically come within days of your request and will spend anywhere from two minutes to two hours, depending on the complexity of the job.

You might be thinking that having a building inspector come to your house during the remodeling is bothersome. Certainly, it will take extra time and will require prior arrangement. (If you are having your apartment installed by a contractor, however, the building inspector's visits will normally be scheduled by the contractor and you may never see the inspector.) Nevertheless, don't think of the building inspector as an enemy, unless of course he or she turns out to be one. Building inspectors can be valuable and inexpensive consultants. Take advantage of any opportunities to ask construction-related questions. Remember that inspectors have a great deal of experience and often give tips worth listening to. However, even if you feel your particular inspector's experience has not increased his or her wisdom, you may want to listen politely anyway, simply because the inspector's approval is quite important to you.

CHAPTER 8

FINDING A CONTRACTOR

Almost anybody installing an accessory apartment will need a contractor at some point, even if he or she is a dedicated do-it-yourselfer. If you have more money than time and skills, you will probably want to turn the whole project over to a general contractor. If you have few technical skills but a lot of ability to work with and manage people, you may want to hire subcontractors and be the general contractor yourself. If you have technical skills and want to do some of the work, such as the carpentry, yourself, you will still need electricians and plumbers, plus a general contractor to supervise the project.

Talking to Contractors

Don't try to save time while looking for contractors. A good contractor will make a difficult project tolerable, while a bad contractor can make an easy project intolerable. The remodeling industry suffers from a bad reputation. There are good contractors out there. The problem is simply how to make sure you find one of them.

Part of the problem is the difference between building something new and rebuilding something old. Any remodeler will tell you that every time you touch an older home you open a Pandora's box of problems that are hard to foresee. This often leads to disagreements between remodelers and homeowners. Contracts are made without taking into account unpleasant surprises, such as old water pipes that crumble into rusty sprinkling systems when disturbed. In such cases it is somehow more satisfying for the homeowner to take his or her frustrations out on the remodeler, and vice versa. Nobody gets much satisfaction from blaming the rust.

One of the differences between a good contractor and one who is just looking for a job is that a good contractor will be very clear with a homeowner about problems that might arise from altering an old home. You may not want to hear what the contractor says about remodeling difficulties you may run into, but you may not have that choice. Your real choice is between hearing about the potential difficulties before you start and being surprised by real difficulties in the middle of the project. A good contractor will warn you beforehand.

Where to Look

The first task in selecting a contractor is to get a good pool of references from which to start. The more you talk with different people about contractors, the more names you will get to pick from, and the better sense you will get of their reputations. Personal friends and business acquaintances are a good place to start because of the frankness of their comments.

Professional organizations of remodelers, who are generally interested in ridding themselves of an unflattering image, often will give referrals of licensed contractors in your area. You may not get the name of the best contractor, but you can be fairly sure you are not getting the worst. The easiest way to get the name of a remodeler's group is to call the local chapter of the National Association of Homebuilders. Typically the local chapters are called something like the Smithtown Homebuilders Association or the Locust County Homebuilders Association. Most of them will have a Remodeler's Council affiliated with them. You can also call the National Association of the Remodeling Industry for references to local chapters. NARI's number, in Arlington, Virginia, is (703) 276-7600.

Your local government's building department can be a good source of references. The more that a local official trusts you not to reveal your source, the better the information you are likely to get. In general it helps to ask questions that the official can answer without appearing to promote one contractor above another. Lumberyards and real estate agents also have experience with contractors and it is always good to talk to them about who does good work. Finally, banks that have special programs for remodeling loans can supply you with the names of the contractors that they know to be reliable.

Preliminary Interviews

Once you have some names of contractors recommended by a couple of sources, ask them to stop by and look at your project. You will want to show them where you think the apartment will be installed, and tell them what it should look like. The clearer you can be about what you want, the more the contractor will be able to tell you about what it might cost. Remember, however, that at this point you don't have to be sure of what you want, and you should feel free to ask the contractor for suggestions and assistance. The contractor is not a consultant to you, but he or she may offer some advice if you ask.

Contractors get business by being asked to make bids on jobs like yours. Their job at this point is to prove to you how good they are by making practical suggestions for improving your plans, by making an educated guess at the cost of the apartment, and, finally, by convincing you that they will be good to work with. If they prove to you how good they are, they know they will be asked to submit a bid. It is in their interest, then, to do a little free consulting.

When you are talking to the general contractor or subcontractor, what do you ask? First, you need to know if he or she can do the job. Find out if he or she has experience doing the kind of job you need done. If you are talking to a general contractor, ask whether or not the contractor has installed an accessory apartment. Ask about jobs that would be similar to installing an accessory apartment, such as converting a garage to living space, or making an unfinished basement into a rec room. If you will need a kitchen and/or a bathroom, does the contractor have experience installing them?

Second, ask the contractor about when he or she could do your job.

If the contractor seems inclined to put your project somewhere at the bottom of a big pile of projects or makes a comment like, "I'm kinda busy, but I'm sure we can squeeze you in somehow," put that down in your mental score sheet as a minus. Typically, a good contractor is busy but knows when time will be available for your job. Remember that a good contractor is worth waiting for.

Third, ask the contractor about his or her history of completing jobs on schedule.

When Are You Ready to Ask for Bids?

Before you ask for bids, you have to know what you want. There is a time for fantasizing about the accessory apartment—when you are planning the apartment, or during your first conversations with contractors. But when you are talking specific tasks, building materials, and prices, you must be pretty definite about what you want. This knowledge will help you get good bids because the contractor will know what precisely he or she is bidding on.

It should be noted here that one of the advantages of hiring an architect is that the architect will provide detailed plans that make it possible for contractors to submit good bids. The architect will also help you select a contractor and will be responsible for supervising the contractor.

Getting a Friend to Help

If you don't have an architect on whom to rely, the experience of finding and working with a contractor is likely to be the most intimidating aspect of installing your accessory apartment. If you feel overwhelmed by it, you should not let yourself be alone in dealing with the contractor.

Find someone who can be with you during the times you are talking to contractors, both during the selection process and during construction. There might be a friend or someone in your family—your spouse, your child, a sibling or parent—who can help you. It should preferably be someone who has experience in construction, and who has time to be a part of the project. If you can't find someone with construction experience, at least have someone else there with whom you can talk easily.

Checking Out a Contractor

There are a number of detailed ways to check up on how good a contractor is. Finding the "best" contractor may be an exercise in frustration. Finding out how to avoid the worst is a much more productive approach. As you begin to think about specific contractors, there are a number of things to consider that can help. A list of them is included below. The list is more of a guide to protecting yourself from bad, "hit-and-run" contractors than to selecting the "best" contractor.

   Does the contractor have an office? A secretary? Has the contractor been at this address for at least a year?

   Has the contractor been in business in the area for at least five years?

   Is the contractor readily able to provide you with references from other jobs he or she has done?

   Has the contractor used high-pressure sales, door-to-door promotions, or phone solicitations as methods of obtaining more clients?

   Is the contractor's bid a hard-to-believe low bid? If so, does he or she have a good explanation of how the job can be done for so little? Have you discussed the low bid and the reasons for it with other people?

   Will the contractor readily give you names of financial institutions with whom he or she does business?

   Are contractors in your community required to have licenses? Does this contractor have one?

Detailed Background Check

Once you have looked at some outward signs of a reputable contractor, look at the financial background of the contractor. One way to start is to see if the contractor has a clean record with the Better Business Bureau and the Consumer Affairs Office. An even better source, however, is any banking institution with which the contractor has carried or currently carries accounts. The question to ask is whether the contractor's financial record is clean of any missed payments.

If you want to do the most thorough check of all, see whether any lawsuits have been filed against the contractor at the local courthouse, and, if so, how they have been resolved.

Visiting a Job Site

Most general contractors will have various projects under way at any one time unless there is a general slow period for the industry. You can visit a contractor's current project and judge for yourself the quality of the work. You might also visit a project that was finished just a short time earlier and talk to the homeowner. Since you probably would not feel comfortable visiting a private home without some introduction, ask the contractor to give you names of other homeowners for whom he or she has recently done work. Then you can call the homeowners. Many will be eager to show off a new remodeling job, particularly if you hint that it sounds attractive or clever from what the builder has told you. Remember, however, that you probably won't want your home to be a showroom once the contractor has finished remodeling it, and maybe the homeowners you have been referred to don't want theirs to be either.

When to Check Out a Contractor in Detail

As you narrow your search for a contractor, you will be trying to uncover more in-depth information about your chief candidates. Don't feel that you have to have the FBI run a security check before you'll even talk to a contractor—not that it isn't a good idea, but being too careful will just take up more time in an already time-consuming process. Wait to do detailed checking until you have one or two contractors in mind and you are close to accepting a bid. Then you should do a really good background check.

Getting Separate Bids

Everybody wants good workmanship at a good price. In practice you have to make some choice between price and workmanship. You cannot expect a contractor to make your accessory apartment a Taj Mahal for the price of building a good doghouse.

The only way for you to be confident that the necessary compromise between price and quality will satisfy you is to have contractors itemize the tasks they will perform and estimate costs for the labor and the materials required to complete the project. That is what you get in a formal bid. If you let the contractors get away with only a verbal estimate, you will have no specific facts about how your money will be spent to incorporate into the contract.

The bid is not considered a contract, nor should it become the contract by itself. When you do hire a contractor, his or her bid will become part of the contract.

The Plans That Are the Basis for Bids

By the time you are ready to ask for bids, you should have had some preliminary talks with contractors, and as a result of those talks, your plans for the apartment should be pretty well defined. If there are one or two decisions that you do not want to make yet, you can ask contractors to give you bids with options. For example, you may want them to give you a price on installing the accessory apartment either with or without a deck attached.

One or two options like this will not be a problem. If you have many options, however, the bidding will become expensive for the contractors, and they may decide that you don't really know what you want and also, perhaps, that you will be hard to deal with. As a result, some contractors may decide to charge you more because they are afraid they will have to absorb some of the costs of dealing with an indecisive client. Other contractors may simply decide not to bid, because it would take up too much of their time to price out the options and might lead to their getting a job they would probably rather not have.

If you are working with an architect, as mentioned earlier, he or she will provide plans that will be the basis for a bid. If you are preparing the plans yourself, you should make a set, the same set, available to all the contractors you ask to bid on the apartment. The plans should contain specific instructions, such as, "Remove partition here," with an arrow pointing to the place on the floor plan where the partition is to be removed. Or, "Remove existing basement window. Enlarge opening and replace with window sized 40″ x 48″; dig out window well and install retaining wall for earth as appropriate." Or, "Install undercounter refrigerator, cooking surface, and microwave in this area."

Plan to get at least three bids on the project. If all of those are disappointing, do not hesitate to call additional contractors for their bids.

Evaluating the Bids

Compare the bids. If all of them are high, try to figure out why. Is there a lot of variation among bids on the costs for the same jobs? Do the inexpensive means of doing the same job look reasonable? If so, then you definitely need additional bids.

If all the bids are high and you can't figure out why, you might ask an architect to look at them as an independent consultant. You will have to pay for this service, but it may be worth it.

Be sure each bid is complete. First, the bid should address labor costs: which types of subcontractors will be employed, at what hourly rates, and for how many hours. Second, the bid should describe the materials that will be used: a description of the material, the quantity to be used, and cost of the material. Third, the bid should give a schedule for completion of the project. Fourth, the bid should describe the terms of a guarantee of workmanship, if the contractor offers such a guarantee.

Your inclination will be to look at the bottom of the bid sheet to "Total Cost." Although this is a major piece of information, it should not be the sole basis of your decision. Consider along with total cost the quality of materials being used and time schedules proposed. Whether or not a guarantee is offered should influence your comparisons. You should also take into account how well you have gotten along with each of the contractors during the process of talking to them and getting bids.

One other major point should be emphasized when you are comparing bids of contractors: Are the contractors bidding on the same project? Have they followed your plans? Make sure that the tasks to be performed are identical in the contractors' bids. If they vary, you are going to have a difficult time trying to compare them.

Contractors may propose a way to do a particular job that is different from what your plans specify. Usually they will do so when they think the job can be done better or cheaper. Make sure that the new proposal is spelled out clearly and itemized in a way that allows you to compare it to the appropriate parts of the other bids. If it is not clear, or if any parts of the bids are not clear, call up the contractor in question and ask for written clarification.

Consider letting each contractor defend his or her bid against the other bids. Don't be afraid to call up the contractor you liked best and say, "Listen, I really liked discussing this project with you, and now I'm trying to make up my mind, but I can't figure out why your total cost

on the kitchen appliances comes out $400 more than the other bids."
Then call up the next contractor and go through the high items in his
or her bid.

How Good Will You Be to Work For?

It has been mentioned that you need a contractor with whom you can
communicate. Now you should think for a moment about how well the
contractor will be able to communicate with you. If you think now about
how well you make decisions and supervise those working for you, you
can avoid problems.

Are You Sure of What You Want?

Avoid rethinking the apartment when it is being built. When the bids
were being made you should have known what you wanted. When the
contract is written up and signed, you must know what you want.

Making last-minute decisions about the work or materials during the
construction phase is going to frustrate your contractor a great deal. Also,
asking that more or less work be done than was initially agreed upon can
be a problem for your contractor. And when it is a problem for your
contractor, it is likely to be a problem for your pocketbook. When you
want to change something in your original plans after the contract is
signed, you cannot easily go and get another contractor, so your contractor has you in a difficult bargaining position. In addition, he or
she may be annoyed that you are making changes that disrupt the
schedule and therefore cost the contractor money. That annoyance will
probably be reflected in the price you get for the changes you are requesting.

Are You Used to Making Decisions?

Deciding whether or not to install an accessory apartment is just the first
in a chain of decisions. Shortly after that one comes the decision of what
contractor to select. During the construction phase you will almost certainly need to make other decisions. The refrigerator you had decided
on will be unavailable. The contractor will discover problems in the
chimney that was going to serve the fireplace in the project. What new

refrigerator will you choose, and how much extra will you spend to have a working fireplace?

Small obstacles routinely appear in construction projects. This is especially true when you open up walls or tamper with heating systems that date from the days of the dinosaurs. How good will you be at deciding how to handle such surprises? In thinking about your answer, remember that many of these construction-related decisions will be new to you. Be prepared to trust your contractor. You will probably have to. This is one of the reasons why, as mentioned earlier, you should not scrimp on time while choosing a contractor.

Will You Pester Your Contractor?

Since you will probably be living in your home during the construction, you will be able to check on how the project is coming along. Now put yourself in the shoes of the contractor. Would you be able to work well if your "boss" was constantly looking over your shoulder? You should observe and ask questions about the project, but not all day long. You must sometimes stand back and let the contractor work. If you feel that you may not be able to resist henpecking the contractor or the workers, then consider a few short trips to distract yourself and get out of your contractor's hair during most of the construction.

Drawing Up a Legal Contract

Incorporating the Bid in a Contract

The information that was supplied in the bid is the groundwork of the contract. However, if you allow the contractor to use the bid as the contract, you are not including in the contract everything that should be agreed upon. The bid is an agreement on what should happen. The contract goes further to include an agreement on what happens in case things don't work out as projected in the bid. The contract should be as comprehensive as possible, including the bid you have accepted as part of it. If necessary, the bid can be modified by mutual agreement between you and the contractor to eliminate all unsatisfactory items or costs and to add specific descriptions of items not detailed sufficiently in the original bid.

Looking for Necessary Clauses

The following is a checklist of clauses that should be included in your construction contract, either as part of the bid or as separate provisions. State or local law may require the inclusion of many of these clauses. You may want to contact your local consumer affairs department for background on laws governing home improvement contracts. In any case, check your contract for the following:

- Specifications of labor time and labor rates.
- Specifications of materials and costs.
- Projected date of completion.
- Method and schedule of payments.
- Requirement that the construction be building-code approved by the local building office before final payment is made.
- Method for charging for changes in construction plans.
- Statement of insurance of contractor for injuries received by workers on the job and for theft or weather damage to materials.
- Requirement for contractor to remove debris following the completion of construction.
- Specification of course of action should either party default, such as a clause stating that you can apply the unpaid portion of the contract to an alternative way of completing the project should the project be delayed unreasonably.
- Specification that if the contractor is arranging for financing for the project, his or her schedule of payments, interest rate, and responsibility in case of default are acceptable to you.

Including Your Side

Construction contracts are drawn up by the contractor. To make life easier on him or her, the contractor may not include some of the above clauses and may try to tell you that they are unnecessary. But the contract is an agreement between the two of you. Just because the contractor wrote the initial contract does not preclude you from adding things. You should add to the contract everything that you consider essential to the success of the contract in guiding the project to meet your specifications. For example, if you insist that the project be completed in two months, make that a part of the contract. If that condition is unacceptable to the contractor, you should know it beforehand. Then, if it is essential to you that the project be completed in two months, you can find another contractor.

Walk Softly But Carry a Big Attorney

It is likely that your construction project will involve a substantial amount of your personal money. In some cases the amount will be as high as thirty or forty thousand dollars. Because the project involves a large amount of money, you should consider having an attorney, an architect, or another building-trades professional read over the contract. Through their experience, they can point out potential problems or omissions. You will probably feel that much more comfortable once you have had the contract reviewed. In addition, you will already know to whom to turn if a problem arises.

Surviving the Construction Phase

Living in a home during remodeling requires the ability to grin and bear it. It is doubtful that you will enjoy your home much while it is torn up. However, it does not have to be extremely unpleasant either. Having good communication with your contractor will make the difference.

Adapting to Schedule Problems

Construction work should be well planned, but room should be left for flexibility when materials do not arrive on time or an unforeseen problem appears. As long as your contractor is exercising proper control over those things that are under his or her supervision, you must learn to relax and be patient. If you think there is a problem, ask the contractor about it early on, so you are not tense. When asking the contractor questions begins to feel like putting bait on the tripping mechanism of a mousetrap, you have waited too long to ask questions. If you aways feel that way, even before work has begun, the problem is probably more yours than the contractor's. As suggested earlier, go away on short trips. You will be taking your problem away with you, to your contractor's benefit and, in the long run, your own.

Working Day-to-Day

Some of the problems that you will experience as you live in your home during the construction phase will be very practical ones. At times the utilities will be turned off. It might be necessary for the water, electricity, or heat to be turned off for a short period of time so that proper connections can be made to the new apartment. To ease the discomfort of that situation, you should ask whether all work necessary on that system can be done at one time so that you do not have the same system shut off more than once. If possible, you may want to have all the systems turned off at once, while you go on a short trip. However, do not get the impression that this is a travel book in disguise. It will be important for you to check up periodically on the work that is being done, particularly if you do not have an architect. You should not go away on long trips, and you should be available to the contractor by phone even when you are off on short ones.

At the very least, you must make sure that the contractor gives adequate warning of when the "shutoff" days will be. This is the kind of thing that you should be able to handle informally.

Other problems of daily life during remodeling are extra noise, fumes in the air, and lack of privacy. If you are at home during the day when the carpenters are working, you might have to adjust to the extra noise in the house. If painting is going on, the fumes can be unpleasant. You might need to leave the house on those days. Finally, it might be frustrating to you to have a lack of privacy in your home while workers are there day in and day out. To help solve any of these problems, you may want to plan to spend as much time as possible in the parts of your house that are furthest from the construction.

When home construction is going on, your house becomes more vulnerable to theft. Many materials are being worked on out-of-doors. Additionally, doors or windows might be removed temporarily, resulting in unsecured access into your home. Therefore, you should take extra precaution during construction to secure materials and tools stored outside and to secure exposed entrances to your home. This is especially critical during the night and while you are away from home.

It is also a good idea to increase, during the construction phase, the amount of fire insurance covering your home. Increased insurance should extend coverage to the materials being used in the remodeling. Also note that the likelihood of fire increases because of the building materials being stored in your yard.

Solving Grievances

If you have followed the steps outlined earlier in choosing a reliable contractor, you have made your best effort to eliminate problems before they arise. But if they do arise, the first action to take is to try to talk it out with the contractor. If the dispute is over materials, the supplier may get involved. Remember, however, that it is the contractor's responsibility to deal with the supplier. You are paying the contractor to take that responsibility and to make sure you get the right materials.

If the dispute is over workmanship, it may involve the subcontractor who did the work. You may want the subcontractor there to find out what really happened and to make sure that the contractor isn't just giving you his or her side of the story. But remember again that you have hired the contractor to make sure the subcontractor gets the job done right.

Remember also that you have an ace up your sleeve in some cases. If the work does not conform to the building code, the building inspector can require the work to be done over.

If you cannot negotiate a settlement with the contractor directly, then contact the agency which licensed the contractor. Often it will be your local consumer protection agency. In any case, the consumer protection agency should be able to help you find out who did license the contractor. It should also be able to help you pursue your complaint. As a last resort, you can take legal action against the contractor through consultation with an attorney and perhaps an architect.

Paying for the Work

The best piece of advice for paying for the work is this: Do not pay all of your money at the beginning of the project. If you pay as the work is completed, you will have leverage with the contractor in making sure that the terms of the agreement are met. In fact, a large final payment is most advantageous to you. This protects you throughout the life of the project against poor workmanship and default by the contractor. As a rule of thumb, you should minimize initial payments and maximize later ones, reserving at least 15 percent for the final payment. The smaller the job, the more you should reserve for final payment. The contract should include a schedule of payments.

Being Your Own General Contractor

The previous discussion assumes that you are planning to hire a general contractor to oversee the entire project. This section considers the possibility of your being the general contractor. The difficulties of the role are discussed elsewhere in some detail, particularly in Chapter 7. This section focuses on practical issues.

Advantages

The biggest advantage to being your own contractor is saving money. As mentioned earlier, the general contractor will usually charge you about 20 percent of the total construction cost for his or her services. That figure will go up or down according to how much troubleshooting the contractor expects to do for your project. If you have an old home in need of improvement, you can expect to pay more for the general contractor's work. If your remodeling project is fairly straightforward, the general contractor's markup may be less than 20 percent.

The other major advantage of being your own general contractor is that you will be in control of the project. You will hire the subcontractors yourself. You will be giving them directives. You will be the one to approve or disapprove their work.

Disadvantages

Being your own general contractor means that you will shoulder the major responsibility of the remodeling project. You will have to dedicate your own time to research the type of design and materials you want, to find and hire subcontractors, and to oversee construction. The headaches caused by scheduling problems, disagreements with building inspectors, and unforeseen problems will be yours. And you will solve disagreements between subcontractors.

Your Biggest Challenge: Coordinating the Subcontractors

In the process of remodeling, tasks must be performed in an orderly fashion. That is not to say, however, that one subcontractor must or even can always complete a task before the next subcontractor begins. Take work on a wall, for example. The carpenter frames the wall. Then the electrician wires the wall. And then the carpenter returns to put up drywall and finish the molding. During this same time you must ensure that the materials needed by the carpenter and electrician will arrive in a timely manner, unless the workers are supplying materials themselves. Now, a wall is only one task, and a simple one at that. In fact, it may be complicated on a large job by bringing in a specialist to put up the drywall, someone who is often known as a "rocker" (from "Sheetrock"). When you try to get a full picture of all the tasks to be accomplished in installing your apartment, you should realize that a task flowchart is required. Without it, you will make expensive mistakes. With it, you may decide that a general contractor is worth the price.

A very general outline of the remodeling process, from the book *Home Remodeling* by A. J. Harmon (Grosset & Dunlap, 1975), is given below:

Masonry work (footings and foundations)

Rough carpentry

Plumbing, electricity

Building inspector's visit

Drywall installation

Sidings, insulation, doors, and windows

Heating and air conditioning ductwork

Finishing work (trim around windows and baseboards, painting, and laying carpet)

Finding Subcontractors

Earlier in this chapter we discussed ways of finding a general contractor. Those guidelines are generally applicable to finding subcontractors as well. To repeat, you should talk to friends, neighbors, and relatives about subcontractors they know. Then you might want to contact labor associations that carry referral lists. Local government building departments are likely to have advice to give. And finally, general contractors or subcontractors in another specialty may give you references.

Dealing with Subcontractors

You should treat each arrangement with a subcontractor as separate from the others. A separate contract, tailored to the situation, should be made with each subcontractor. Not all of your subcontractors will do business the same way.

When the construction is under way, you will need to supervise the subcontractors. You must be attentive but not overbearing. You will also want to pay the subcontractor on a schedule. Reserve as much as possible for the final payment for the same reasons discussed above.

Hiring Subcontractors and Workers

If you hire electricians, carpenters, and plumbers, you might be considered an employer under some tax codes. The IRS requires you to register as an employer if the project is more than short-term and if you are setting strict work schedules for the workers. State laws are similar, but you must take time to investigate them.

The issue of directly hiring workers raises other issues. If you are an employer, you are normally responsible for withholding taxes, disability insurance, and workers' compensation. The added expense is one problem, but the added risk is an even greater one. If someone is hurt working for you, you could be sued for enough to take care of him or her while disabled. To be sure about the laws in your state, contact the state department of labor. Another good place to turn for advice, and coverage, is your insurance agent.

TAKING SERVICES AS RENT

Once you have your apartment installed, you need to find a tenant. Chapter 10 discusses how to find a tenant. First, however, it is important to think about what kind of tenant you want.

Installing an accessory apartment in your home can do more for you than bring in rent. You may be able to find a tenant willing to provide services in exchange for a reduction in rent. Also, as a homeowner, you may want to provide some services to your tenant, either to increase your income or to get additional services yourself.

What Services to Exchange

Household Maintenance

Household maintenance services are the type of service most frequently provided in a service exchange. Most people can do a competent job of household maintenance, so providers of household maintenance services are the easiest to find.

Household maintenance includes so many tasks that you have to be very specific in the terms of your agreement. The amount and the kind of assistance depend on the quality of the apartment you are offering and the reduction in rent. In most cases, for example, you should not expect a person to agree to do all your housework. But you probably can arrange to have specific jobs done, such as washing windows or waxing floors. Other kinds of household jobs often covered by service-exchange agreements include lawn mowing, snow shoveling, putting up screens and storm windows, leaf raking, and taking out garbage cans.

Beware of what is frequently called the "live-in maid syndrome." It is the assumption that, in return for housing, some poor, miserable person will be willing to become your indentured servant. A tenant rarely will, and the assumption that he or she might tends to give the homeowner a series of unstable and unhappy tenants, and endless frustration.

Security

One of the most valuable services a tenant can provide is "being there." If you have an accident, someone is close at hand. If a burglar breaks into your home, your tenant can call the police. When you go on vacation, your tenant can turn lights on at night so that it looks like someone is at home. In fact, someone is at home!

Many older people in particular feel the need for this kind of security. Older people in precarious health who live alone without much social contact can have an accident or health emergency without anyone knowing about it until the situation is critical. For that reason, social service programs have sprung up for the sole purpose of checking on people on a regular basis. A tenant in an accessory apartment can provide that same service for you.

You can arrange to have your tenant call you or drop by every day to make sure you are okay. Or, you can have your tenant work in conjunction with an established social service program for checking on older people. The program could take over on the tenant's day off, or your tenant could be contacted to follow up if you could not be reached for your check-in telephone call: Were you too ill to answer the phone, or did you forget about your regular call and go for a walk?

Single parents, who nine times out of ten are women, and women living alone often have as much concern about security as the elderly. Having someone next door can add a great deal of comfort.

As with household work, it is important to define what kind of security you expect. If you expect your tenant to be there every night, or every night when you are on vacation, or simply most of the time, these expectations should be defined and included in your lease.

Transportation

It's hard to imagine a place to live where you don't have to drive at all. In some cities you can get by on public transportation, but most of the people who can afford to live there, except for the very poor, don't get by on public transportation alone. In most suburbs and rural areas, you just have to get around by car.

What happens if you are no longer able to drive or if the spouse on whom you depended for transportation has died or is no longer there because of a divorce? Situations of this kind force many people to leave a home where they would otherwise stay.

Transportation is a service that a tenant in an accessory apartment can provide. Like arrangements for household maintenance services, you can either arrange a plan of rides, such as one weekly trip to the grocery store and one monthly trip to the doctor, or arrange a certain amount of time to be spent on transportation, such as 10 hours per month.

If you have your own car, you may not have to reduce the rent much in exchange for transportation. The reduction may be even smaller if you allow the tenant to make personal use of your car for a certain number of hours per week. Older people who have cars they no longer want to maintain, and others who simply find car maintenance an aggravation, may also want to make the tenant responsible for having the car serviced.

It is also possible that you can get a tenant who will provide a car. In this case, you may have to allow a more substantial rent reduction, depending on how often you need transportation services. However, you will save the cost and problems of keeping a car.

Child Care

For some parents caught in the complications of a daily trip from home to day care to work and back again, having a baby-sitter in the home is a dream come true. It can also be a blessing to have someone who is not specifically a baby-sitter, but is simply there when school-age kids come home.

We all know that there are a lot of working mothers. At least half of the women with children under 6 are in the work force today. This translates into a tremendous need for day care, particularly if you also consider the number of children over 6 who are still not old enough to care for themselves after school is out. In the face of this need, having a tenant who can help take care of the kids can make life much easier.

If you need to find day care for your children, consider renting your accessory apartment to someone who can give you that service. A good choice might be a single parent who wants to stay at home with his or her own children. Although it is reported that many older people dread the idea of starting a second career as a baby-sitter, not all old people do. You might find a retired person who would love to take care of children, particularly if his or her responsibilities were clearly defined so that it did not become a second career.

If you are a parent who only occasionally needs baby-sitting services, you would probably find it much more convenient to have a baby-sitter right in the house, who is simply there, who expects to baby-sit frequently, who is well known by the kids, and who doesn't have to be picked up just when you are rushing to get ready for a party.

If you are a homeowner who likes children, it is also worth remembering that a homeowner with an accessory apartment can also give day care. For example, an older woman who offered an accessory apartment and assistance in day care would probably get an enormous response from single parents. If you can offer a nice place to live and day care to a single parent, you have a lot of bargaining power. That could be used either to get additional rental income, or to get a combination of rent and services you need.

Personal Care and Nonintrusive Medical Care

The term "personal care" encompasses such services as helping a person dress, helping a person with limited mobility get around, and helping a person take medications. Many frail elderly people need this help very badly, and many not so badly, but all of those who need it will have a much more enjoyable life if the help is available.

This kind of service is so personal and intimate that many people feel uncomfortable providing it. In addition, the provider of personal care services has a serious responsibility that is different from other types of service exchanges. It's one thing for a tenant to forget to mow the lawn. It's quite another to forget to help a person out of bed. However, if you need this kind of service, it is still possible to get it, or some of it, through a service exchange.

The same is true of some levels of medical assistance. There are many medical procedures and treatments that can easily be taught to a layperson. Of course, any intrusive or "hands-on" medical care must be left to professionals, but a properly trained tenant can help with simple medical procedures. Training of home care-givers is provided nationally by the American Red Cross, and in some areas by hospitals or other groups formed for the specific purpose of encouraging home care as opposed to institutional care.

If you, your elderly parents who live in a single-family home, or some other relative need this kind of help, discuss the situation with a doctor or a visiting nurse. If he or she agrees that a person with some training could help, consider the possibility of finding a tenant willing to provide the services. If you set up a service exchange of this kind, do so with the help or supervision of someone with medical training, such as a doctor or registered nurse.

It might be convenient to have someone giving you this kind of assistance live in the same home with you. However the person would be giving up so much independence and privacy that, in addition to your loss of privacy, you would lose a great deal of the economic benefit from providing the person with housing. If the service provider had his or her own unit, however, your bargaining power would be much stronger.

In this connection it is worth noting that a household matching service in Grand Junction, Colorado, located in the Hilltop House Rehabilitation Hospital, specializes in structuring service exchanges of this type for people who are being discharged from hospitals. A household matching service is an agency that specializes in finding compatible tenants for people who want to rent out a room. They are explained in more detail in Chapter 10, which also includes information on how to find them. Some of these agencies assist in structuring service exchanges, but few are set up to arrange service exchanges that involve personal care and nonintrusive medical care. However, they are the best place to start if you are going to set up a service exchange of this kind.

Service Management by a Tenant

Suppose you or a relative is among the very frail elderly who need a wide variety of services to be independent and stay in their own homes. An alternative to having a tenant who provides services is having a tenant who manages services.

In your community there are almost certainly various organizations available to provide you with in-home services. There is one organization that will deliver your meals. There's another that provides a visiting nurse. There's another that gives you rides to your doctor and church. You may have no trouble managing the services you receive, but many people find it difficult to arrange services for themselves. There are forms to fill out and calls to make and appointments and medications to keep straight. In addition, you may not be in a position to check up on the quality of service you are getting. It can be complicated and exhausting.

The one service you may require from your tenant, then, is to manage your services for you. Let your tenant make the calls to arrange transportation or find out what happened when your meals stopped coming. Set the tenant up as a kind of live-in lawyer to take your side for you. Again, a service like this will require clear definition of the time required from the tenant, and of the kinds of things he or she should manage. It is the kind of role a college student or a confident older person could handle well. And it also must be someone you trust. The next sections discuss how to find a tenant you can rely on and trust.

Finding a Tenant to Provide Service Exchanges

Who Is Willing to Trade Services for Housing?

Most tenants of accessory apartments want a place to live for a fair price, with no complications. But some people who need a place to live have extra time or energy and limited incomes. For them, it makes sense to trade some of their time or energy for a place to live or a reduction in rent. Two groups of people are typically in this situation: college students and the "young elderly" in their fifties and sixties with moderate incomes.

College students tend to have flexible schedules and extra energy. They are also usually in a financial pinch and like to "swing deals" to get by. Independent Living of Madison, Wisconsin, is a household matching program that specializes in setting up service exchanges between college students and elderly people. The students have proved to be good service providers in return for housing. Another good thing about college students is that there are a lot of them. It is surprising how many college towns there are.

The second group of potential service providers, the young elderly, have typically retired young. They may have some extra time, and they are often single and living on limited incomes. These are usually people who are used to work, to taking responsibility, and to making decisions. The problem is that you may have trouble finding someone in this category.

Single parents with young children are another potential source of help in a service exchange. Many divorced or widowed mothers with young children find themselves in greatly reduced financial circumstances compared to their married years. Many of them want to stay at home with their children and therefore may have very small incomes. They need to find an inexpensive place to live that is also a good place to raise children. An exchange of services for a reduction in rent can make this possible. Remember, however, that a single parent will almost always want an apartment with at least two bedrooms.

The ease with which you can find a tenant willing to provide services in exchange for a reduction in rent depends in part on what services you need. Personal care providers are the hardest to find. On the other hand, there are some people who prefer to provide personal services over other kinds of services. Some people feel that by providing personal services they are really helping someone with something important. For some, often women, taking care of others is the most developed skill they have and the one in which they feel the most confidence.

Even if you find a tenant who wants to provide personal care services, you may find that you have to do more than reduce the rent, depending on the amount of services you want. You may have to pay a salary in addition to providing housing. This may work to your advantage, because a person who is receiving a salary has accepted a more formal commitment to work for you. However, the salary does not have to be for full-time work, and probably should not be in many cases. If it is, it will turn the service exchange into a job and may discourage some potential tenants who do not want to see themselves as servants of some kind.

Special Advantages You Can Offer Tenants

In one study, a tenant in an accessory apartment was interviewed just after he had helped the man he rented from dig out a clogged sewer line.

He had given the help voluntarily, and he said he was always willing to help voluntarily—when the decision to help was his. A service exchange would take the decision out of his hands. He didn't want to come home from an intense job and have other responsibilities to face. The same will be true of many people. Tenants for service-exchange situations will often be harder to find.

On the other hand, you probably can offer more enticements to potential tenants than you think. For example, two things apartment dwellers often dream of having are a workshop and a garden. Can you offer either? Could you let a tenant work on a car in your garage? Could you set aside a portion of your yard for your tenant's use as a private yard or garden? Are you willing to accept large pets? Your first step in setting up a service exchange is recognizing that accessory apartments can offer advantages that other types of rental housing do not.

You can use these advantages in your advertising to attract more applicants. However, some of them will obviously be advantages only to individuals with specific interests or characteristics. If you are willing to let a tenant have occasional use of your car as part of the service exchange, that will be a big advantage to some people, but obviously only to those who don't have cars. In many cases you may have to meet potential tenants and talk to them about their individual interests before you can suggest the kind of arrangement that would work best for both you and the tenant. When you are talking to potential tenants, find out as much about them as you can, and then see what you can offer them above and beyond the accessory apartment itself.

Chapter 10 discusses how to find a tenant for your accessory apartment. The advice in that chapter on how to advertise for a tenant applies as well to finding a tenant when you wish to set up a service exchange. However, included below are suggestions on how to find a tenant who is willing to exchange services. Many of these suggestions are developed further in Chapter 10.

Where to Advertise

Where to advertise for likely tenants depends on whom you want for a tenant. You would probably be most comfortable with a tenant who comes with a personal recommendation by someone you know, so start talking to people you know. Talk to neighbors, friends, people at your place of worship or other places where you know people. Does anyone have a niece moving into town to go to college? Or a daughter who has a young child, is recently separated from her husband, and needs a place to live? Does anyone know a person recently retired who needs to adjust to a reduced income? People like to help, so give them a chance to.

If you can't find someone through your circle of acquaintances, start looking for people in places where the kind of tenant you want is likely to be. If you want a college student, contact local colleges. Almost all colleges have a housing office for students and a job office for students. Contact both. You will probably be asked to fill out a card to be posted on a bulletin board. You can also run an ad in the student paper.

If you want to find a retired person, you will have to break into the network of services for older people. If you already have a contact, start with that person. You may be familiar with a senior center in your area, or a senior housing program. Contact someone there and explain your needs. Many areas have catalogs of senior organizations that include service descriptions. Contact groups that sound appropriate.

If you don't have any contact with places that provide services to older persons, you should start with your local government. You should be able to find an Agency on Aging or an Office on Aging. They are frequently housed within the social services branch of local governments. Staff in those offices should be able to refer you to the kind of organization you are looking for.

Single parents might be tricky to find, but well worth it if your need is for baby-sitting services. Try contacting day-care centers. Ask if you can post a notice of what you need. The center may already have a mechanism for exchanging information, such as a bulletin board or newsletter.

Classified advertisements in newspapers are a good source of tenants for service exchanges. If you run an ad in the apartments section, detail the advantages of the apartment as well as the extent of the services you require. Two sections you should check are "Roommate wanted" and "Positions wanted." You can run an ad in "Roommate wanted," "Apartment, rooms, houses to share," or "Domestic help wanted." Often people looking to share an apartment would much rather have an apartment of their own and would be willing to provide some services in order to get one. Your local newspapers might have other listings that you should consider. Read all the sections in your paper that might do, and decide which is best for your advertisement.

Household Matching Services

Chapter 10 gives information on how to find and use a household matching service. As mentioned earlier, these are services that typically find compatible tenants for people who want to rent a room in their houses. Often in doing so they structure service exchanges. Most metropolitan areas have them.

If there is more than one agency in your area, try to find out which agency has done the most work in setting up service exchanges. Information on how to find these agencies and what to expect from them is treated in more detail in Chapter 10.

How to Choose a Tenant

Once you have some prospective tenants, you will have to choose which one is best for you. Consider the situation objectively, then go with your personal inclination—that is, choose the person you like even if his or her score is not the best on your checklist of tenant qualities. Don't ignore objective qualifications for the job, but once you have narrowed the field to acceptable applicants, then choose the one who appeals to you personally. Remember, in most cases, you will be having a personal relationship with this person. A good relationship may be more important than the quality of the services themselves.

A few examples may clarify this advice. You want a tenant who will pay the rent and take care of the yard. In this situation it doesn't seem very important that you also personally like the person, since you won't be dealing with him or her all that often. As long as you don't dislike any of your prospective tenants, choose the one with the best record of being responsible.

On the other hand, suppose you are an older person who needs someone to help you dress and prepare your meals. You are going to have a close relationship with this person. Suppose that your choice of tenants includes a widow who has little experience helping adults dress and a retired registered nurse who has a great deal of professional experience in just what you need. If you like the widow a great deal more than the nurse, choose the widow. In this case your personal feelings toward the person should win out over professional experience. Also, as noted below, it may be possible for your tenant to get some inexpensive training in how to help you.

Striking a Fair Bargain

Whatever combination of services and housing is being exchanged, it has to be seen as fair for both parties. It's important to recognize that if either you or your tenant feels taken advantage of, the service exchange is not going to work.

A principle to start off with is that you shouldn't bargain too hard. A hard-driven bargain very often means one in which one or both of the bargainers have been forced to compromise. If you find yourself losing out on what you want from a service exchange, stop negotiating. Start again with a new person. You don't want someone around helping you who you feel is taking advantage of you. Similarly, you don't want someone helping who feels you are taking advantage of him or her all the time.

Minimizing Tenant Turnover

Unhappy tenants will leave. A high turnover in tenants is bad news for you in most cases. It may cost you money and effort every time you search for a new tenant. The best way to minimize tenant turnover is to think about the potential tenant's own view of the future. To do this you should do the same thing you should do when trying to attract a tenant. Take some extra time when interviewing the tenant to find out what his or her hopes for the future are. If they include having a big vegetable garden, and you can make that possible, then the relationship will have a better chance of working. If the tenant hopes to go on a diet to lose 50 pounds, attend night school to get a degree in international finance while working a full-time job, and also provide you with hot meals every night, he or she may scarcely have time in practice to worry about his or her own hot meals, let alone yours.

Consider another situation. Suppose you find somebody to pay a high rent for your accessory apartment and still provide you with services. Someone in a tight situation might agree to that kind of a deal, but that person will leave as soon as a better deal comes along. Tenants who feel that they're getting their money's worth won't be looking for a better deal. In general, even though it is hard to find tenants for a service exchange situation, do not take someone who is really in need of charity unless he or she has more than good looks to indicate reliability.

Sometimes tenants are so happy about their arrangement that they will go to great lengths to please the homeowner. One tenant in Westport, Connecticut, repeatedly offered to pay more rent because she liked the apartment so much she wanted to be sure the owners didn't decide not to rent it anymore. The homeowner was already satisfied and refused to accept the increased rent, so the tenant finally bought the homeowner a new washing machine. The homeowner was happy to accept the new washer, and the tenant felt more secure than ever with her living arrangements.

In spite of what was said earlier about the problems of high tenant turnover, even with fair and carefully planned agreements some tenants may not stay long in service exchange arrangements. Many tenants who enter into a service exchange are at a pivotal point in their lives, such as just being divorced, or just widowed. Many are college students who are only in town for the school year. They are in situations that require frequent reevaluation until they settle into a new role. So, after about six or eight months, tenants of this kind will move on to something new. If it sounds discouraging, you shouldn't assume it necessarily means a hard situation for you as a landlord. Often these are the people who better themselves because they do a pretty good job of whatever they take on.

There are many people of this type in the Washington, D.C., area who seek housing on a temporary basis for six or eight months. Often they are people who have come to the area hoping to get a good job and make a start. Some statistics from the area's household matching service indicate that homeowners who had tenants for this length of time did not seem to mind the relatively short length of the tenancy. Although the statistics are not directly applicable because they refer to homeowners who rented rooms, generally without service exchanges, they show that short-term tenants can be good tenants. Eighty-five percent of the homeowners in the study returned to the household matching service for new tenants when the initial tenants left. Many homeowners like the sense that they will always be getting to know new people.

Changing the Terms of Trade

You should be willing to adjust the terms of trade as needs change. Both you and your tenant need to be flexible. Suppose your tenant has agreed to take care of your kids every Saturday morning while you go to the grocery store and run other errands. You discover that Saturday morning is the worst time to do grocery shopping. Discuss with your tenant what other times would be convenient for him or her to help. It could be that Saturday morning wasn't the tenant's first choice anyway.

You also have to take into account that your tenant's needs may change. For example, if your tenant is a college student, his or her schedule is going to change every term. If your tenant originally agreed to baby-sit for your children every Thursday night, that deal might be impossible when he or she has to take a class that is offered only Thursday evenings. You don't have to give up your night out; you just have to make it another day of the week. Both you and your tenant will be happier if your arrangement is flexible. Remember, however, that flexibility is no substitute for the kind of clear definition of responsibilities mentioned earlier.

Giving the Tenant Respite

If your tenant is providing you with much in the way of services, and working at a full-time job as well or going to school full-time, he or she is going to need time off, or what in the field of caregiving for the elderly is called "respite." Be careful not to turn your tenant's life into a literally full-time job or an endurance test. Take a tip from the professionals. The household matching service in Wisconsin mentioned earlier will no longer set up service-exchange matches unless respite is included as part of the contract for service exchanges. Regular respite for your tenant should be included as part of your bargain. Think of respite as insurance that your tenant will remain satisfied and on the job.

One easy way to build respite into the service exchange is to have more than one tenant. That way, they can spell each other or divide the work between them. Of course, you would need an apartment big enough for two people, and the two tenants would have to work well together. You could also have one tenant in an apartment and one renting a room in your part of the house.

If two people have agreed to provide personal care services, then neither tenant has an overwhelming job. They can alternate days or tasks so that days off are frequent or tasks are minimal. If you have two providers sharing the work, you may not have to pay a salary to either provider.

Another way to provide respite for your tenant is to use the tenant in conjunction with other service providers. For example, in many areas

Meals on Wheels are delivered only Monday through Friday. If you need help with meal preparation, you could use Meals on Wheels Monday through Friday and ask your tenant to provide meals only on weekends. Or you may have a relative or friend who is happy to help you out on weekends but works during the week. You could have your tenant help you during the week and give the tenant weekends off when other people can help you out.

Initiate a Service Exchange Before You Need It

Service exchanges can be especially valuable for many elderly persons. The fastest-growing age group in the country is people over 75. Many of these people are at risk of being forced to leave their homes and possibly enter institutions. Why would someone unwillingly leave their home? The answer is usually that, because of a chronic illness, they are unable to maintain the home, either financially or physically, or are unable to meet their own personal needs. For example, a person who has suffered a stroke may be left with partial paralysis leading to an inability to dress or drive. Without some sort of help in the home, such people have to move to a place where there is someone to help them dress and someone to manage all their needs that require a car, such as buying food.

It used to be true that there were many people in nursing homes who did not need to be there but were forced to move into that kind of totally dependent living situation because of an inability to be totally independent. There are still many cases like this. However, because of stricter rules by insurance companies and the federal government, it does not happen as often. What still can happen is that, because of an inability to be totally independent, an individual will deteriorate. For example, the person will not be able to bathe or clean the house. This leads to infections and illnesses that become increasingly severe, so that the person eventually does need the care of a nursing home.

There is a growing recognition of the need to avoid this kind of tragic decay in health by providing care in the home. There are many programs providing such care, but they are often linked to a need for skilled nursing care or other medical care. For example, if all you need is help cleaning your house and help with transportation, you may be ineligible for some programs. Other programs that provide in-home services have income restrictions so that only people with very low incomes will be eligible. Many people "fall through the cracks" of these programs because they are neither sick nor poor enough.

But in addition to those who are not served because of program limitations, there are those who postpone getting the kind of assistance that a service exchange makes possible because they believe that getting the assistance in itself will crystallize the aging process. It will make them feel weaker.

In fact, this view is close to saying that being independent means being isolated. The real skill and the real ability to control your own future, at any age, depends on the ability to work well with other people so that you get the services you need. Postponing an accessory apartment and a service exchange, as a single parent or a working couple or an empty nester or a frail elderly person, when it makes economic sense, can often mean you are weaker as a person. You are weaker not because you need help, but because when there is a way to make life better you do not take it.

The kinds of services you might want have already been detailed. Think carefully about what your future looks like. Most women over age 75 live alone. Do you see that for yourself? Or your wife? Consider the possibility that you might need in-home services in the future. Do you have a network of family and friends who can help you? If you don't, or if you're not sure, or if you don't want to be a burden to them, consider what an accessory apartment could do for you in the future. It could be that all you would get out of having an accessory apartment is extra income. Or you may, like many people, find that it makes an enormous difference in the quality of your life.

Harry and Sally are a good example of a successful service exchange. They live in New Haven, Connecticut. He owns the home, is 93, and loses his balance occasionally. His sons did not want him to live alone. He found Sally. She is 57. She works full time outside the home but does all Harry's housework and cooks dinner for him. She gets free rent and use of the house and garage, and she has a whole lot more money to spend because she does not have to pay rent. For both of them, it is more than a service exchange. According to Sally, "It's a kind of instant family."

Writing a Service Exchange into a Lease

The best type of lease to use in a service exchange is a combination of a standard lease, modified for an accessory apartment as discussed in Chapter 10, and a written service-exchange agreement. The written service-exchange agreement will be discussed here.

A Specific and All-Inclusive Agreement

The service exchange agreement should be part of the lease for the apartment. It should not be a separate document. After all, the deal is for housing and services, not just one or the other. It should be clear, if the services are important to you, that failure to perform the services agreed to is a violation of the lease and sufficient cause for the homeowner to terminate it.

The agreement for services can be written either as a statement or as a checklist of services. The Shared Housing Resource Center, Inc., of Philadelphia includes this statement in the lease, followed by several blank lines: "The Homesharer shall provide the following services in lieu of $____ of the monthly rent (be specific and include frequency)." Another household matching agency uses a checklist. Here is part of the list.

	HOMEOWNER	TENANT
Room	_____	_____
Board	_____	_____
Yard work	_____	_____
Days off	_____	_____

Both methods have advantages and disadvantages. When only one or two services are required from the tenant, the statement method is a good choice. The blank lines can be filled in with a statement such as "Mow the lawn once per week from the first week of April until the last week of October unless the homeowner agrees it is not necessary." The checklist method is a better choice if the tenant is going to provide several services. You can list all the services to be exchanged and then note the frequency or amount under the column of the person providing the service. For example, across from Yard work under Tenant you would note "Mow lawn once per week April–October."

It's important to write everything down. The lease formats given above are very simple compared to the information that should actually be included. In writing up the service-exchange agreement, be sure to think up problems that might lead to misunderstandings. Does "cooking meals" mean hot meals? Does it mean three times a day? Does providing security mean being there 365 days a year? Does it mean being in before 10 p.m. every night?

If your tenant agrees to move heavy objects occasionally or get things out of the attic, don't let that stand as a verbal agreement only. Make a heading on your checklist for moving heavy objects and note a frequency that you two can agree on, such as half an hour per week or one hour per month. Iron out all the details in writing so you both know exactly what to expect. The purposes of a detailed written agreement are to minimize misunderstandings and to provide a record to which to refer if misunderstandings do occur.

Insurance Coverage

Liability is a four-letter word, but you have to think about it. Appropriate insurance coverage is a must for all service-exchange agreements. In most cases the homeowner's insurance will cover accidents and liability in the home for both the homeowner and the tenant, but be certain! Check with your insurance agent and explain the situation, including what services the tenant will be giving to you.

You should be aware that household matching services are not responsible for any liability resulting from your sharing of a common residence. In fact, you will very likely be required to sign a release of liability from the agency helping you find a tenant.

CHAPTER 10

THE LAST STEP:
SELECTING A TENANT

Many people are nervous about the idea of selecting a tenant. Actually, they are nervous about selecting the wrong tenant.

To start with, they are nervous about the questions they want to ask prospective tenants. The trouble with most of these questions is that they are probing and personal and not questions most of us would ask in everyday life. You don't normally ask people right after meeting them if they play loud music or use drugs. However, these are questions many homeowners want to ask. Not only that, they want to ask the questions and at the same time make prospective tenants feel at ease. They want to make them feel at ease because if they are feeling nervous and backed up against the wall it is hard to find out whether or not they will be good to have as close neighbors. It is the kind of situation in which years of diplomatic training are about as helpful as a bathing suit in a blizzard.

Along the same lines, many people are nervous about asking for and checking references. People unused to business dealings often feel that asking someone for references implies you already think the person is questionable.

If you would feel nervous about this, the best thing to do is use a tenant finding service, or, as they are more commonly called, a household matching service. The next best thing to do is to follow guidelines for finding tenants set up by people with experience in doing so. The first section of this chapter goes into how to find and use a household matching service. The second section summarizes the information available on how to find a good tenant yourself.

Regardless of how you go about selecting a tenant, three principles apply. These will be spelled out in more detail below, but they are stated here as the guiding lights of tenant selection. First, be as clear as you can about what you expect of your tenant. Second, put those expectations in a written contract. After you have carefully applied the first and second principles, apply the third: Keep one eye half shut.

Household Matching Services

Household matching services are a relatively new institution. Their basic function is not to help people find tenants for accessory apartments; they started to help promote shared housing. Shared housing is what would have been known forty or fifty years ago as taking in a lodger. It was and often still is called renting out a room. At its best, it creates, in the words of the National Shared Housing Resource Center, a "family of choice."

Nationally, the number of household matching services has gone from about 50 in 1980 to about 380 in 1984, according to the National Shared Housing Resource Center. Although they were not started specifically to help find tenants for accessory apartments, to most household matching services an accessory apartment is not that different from shared housing. In fact, accessory apartments are often considered a form of shared housing. A household matching service has as its goal setting up matches between people who are compatible enough to enjoy sharing the same house. This typically means sharing the TV and the kitchen and the chores and sometimes the bathroom. As a homeowner with an accessory apartment, you will not be sharing the same living unit, so you will not be sharing any of those things. Nonetheless, it will be nice to have a tenant chosen with the same care.

How to Find One

As indicated by the growth in household matching services mentioned above, they now exist in most major metropolitan areas. Most of them are nonprofit. Typically, these matching agencies are not well known. They get an initial burst of publicity and then, after it fades, never get well known. The easiest way to locate them is by calling a local government housing, social services, or aging agency. Generally household matching services have names like Operation Match, Share-A-Home, or Project Share. It is often possible to locate them through local government general-purpose information and referral numbers as well. You can also write to the National Shared Housing Resource Center, Inc., at 6344 Greene Street, Philadelphia, PA 19144. This center sells a *National Directory of Shared Housing Programs* for $4.50. The price includes postage and handling.

What to Look For

You should know what to expect in the way of services from a household matching agency. The National Shared Housing Resource Center divides matching services into two main types: referral agencies and counseling agencies. The difference is in the degree to which someone from the service gets to know both homeowners looking for tenants and tenants looking for housing.

In a counseling agency, someone from the agency will interview both the homeowner and the tenant, often in their own homes. Someone from the agency will also be there when the homeowner and tenant first meet. On the other hand, a referral agency will usually collect information over the phone. Most agencies fall somewhere between the two types.

As a homeowner, you would be asked by either type of agency about the kind of person you are looking for, the kind of place you are renting, whether or not you accept pets, dislike smokers, etc. You will also be asked what personal interests you have and so forth, right down to, in one case, the temperature you prefer to keep your house. Tenants are asked corresponding questions. Both tenants and homeowners will be asked for references, and in most cases those references will be checked. However, it is a good idea to ask specifically whether a prospective tenant's references have been checked.

The matching agency uses all this information to propose a suitable tenant for the homeowner. Staff people become quite skilled at suggesting compatible matches. Some now use computer programs to assist them in initial comparisons of the information they have collected on home-owners and tenants. Obviously, if you are a homeowner who is nervous about finding a good tenant, the availability of a household matching agency will be a big advantage to you. In fact, if finding a good tenant is your worst worry about installing an accessory apartment, you may want to make finding a household matching agency your first step. If you find one, call them up and talk to them. Get them to send you some literature, and go visit them and see whether you trust them. If you don't trust them, or if a household matching agency is not available, you may want to decide not to install an apartment.

One example of the way in which such agencies help is indicated by how the homeowner and tenant proposed for a match are brought to-gether. Typically, the agency gives out telephone numbers, not addresses. You, as homeowner, will typically get a call from the agency describing a potential tenant. If the person sounds good to you, the agency will ask him or her to call you. When you feel comfortable over the phone, you can give out your address. You do not have to worry about having a stranger you feel uncomfortable with coming to your house.

Another good thing about nonprofit household matching agencies is how inexpensive they are. Some charge nothing at all, and most charge very low fees for their services. For example, the household matching service in Philadelphia, called Philadelphia Match, charges $5 when you apply to find a tenant and $20 when a tenant is found and accepted. Such fees are less than a tenth of what it costs the matching agency to put together a good match. Volunteers often do much of the work. Fees will probably increase in the future, but even so the assistance of a matching agency will be a bargain.

Private Agencies

There are also private referral agencies that can find tenants for you. As a group, they have the reputation of providing uneven service. From your point of view as a homeowner, it is important to remember that they do not have the flexibility of nonprofit household matching agencies. If they take a great deal of time with any individual client, they lose money on that client. They therefore often cannot take the time required to address individual concerns. While nonprofit matching agencies cannot afford to spend enormous amounts of time with any individual household, they often can be more flexible.

Real estate agents who manage property also can often be used as a source of tenants. For a fee, they will often be willing to take on the problem of selecting a tenant for your final approval. However, for some homeowners, an even bigger advantage will be that the real estate agent can manage the apartment for you for a monthly fee or percentage of the rent. This means that any complaints about leaky plumbing or peeling paint go to the real estate agent first. The agent may provide an ongoing maintenance service as part of the package. The price will not always be cheap, but for many people, particularly someone who is quite old, such a service will be a big advantage. All the worries about collecting the rent each month and so forth are passed on to someone else.

Whether or not having someone manage the apartment makes sense to you will depend on what you want out of it. If your main interest is income, it will probably not make sense to have it managed by a real estate agent. If you want a little extra income, plus the security of having someone right next door, then it probably will make sense.

This kind of arrangement may also be a big advantage to "snowbirds." Snowbirds are best known in the midwest but are common to all the snow-covered regions of the country. They are people who go south for the winter. If you are a snowbird, or would like to become one, an accessory apartment managed by a real estate agent is a very good way to keep the family home without spending your time in the sunshine worrying about burst pipes and leaky roofs. You will have a tenant in the house paying you for the privilege of keeping an eye on things. And the tenant will have someone else to call when problems crop up.

Finding a Tenant on Your Own

If there isn't a matching service you can use, or if you don't want to use one, there are several good guides you can use to select a tenant by yourself. One is *Living With Tenants* by Doreen Bierbrier (McGraw-Hill, 1986). Ms. Bierbrier articulated the "keep one eye half shut" principle described earlier. Another, by the National Shared Housing Resource Center, is entitled *Home Sharing Self-Help Guide*, and can be ordered as follows:

National Shared Housing Resource Center
6344 Greene Street
Philadelphia, PA 19144
Enclose $2.75 for postage and handling.

Both of these guides address shared living. However, all it takes to apply them to an accessory apartment situation is to skip some parts that are irrelevant, such as deciding whether or not the TV will be shared. *Living With Tenants* is more detailed than *Home Sharing Self-Help Guide*, but it is also more expensive. Both go into more detail than it is possible to include in this book.

Defining Your Expectations

As mentioned earlier, one of the principles of a successful relationship with a tenant is a clear definition of expectations. How do you go about defining your own expectations of a tenant? The process is not that hard. Write down all the obvious things you want or do not want in an ideal tenant. Here is a checklist drawn in part from the two sources mentioned above.

- Will you permit smoking?
- Will you permit pets?
- Will you permit a loud stereo?
- Will you permit an occasional party? How often is "occasional"?
- Will you permit overnight guests of the opposite sex if your tenant is single?
- Will you permit any use of drugs?
- How many cars will you provide parking for?
- Will you permit the tenant to use the yard, and if so, will you define portions of it for your exclusive use or the tenant's?
- Will you mind someone who has odd working hours?
- Will you want someone who is out of the house during working hours so you can feel you have the house to yourself at times?
- Will you require someone who has a full-time job or other stable source of income?

- Will you permit water beds?
- Will you permit children, and if so, how many?

Getting Ready to Advertise

In addition to thinking of all the expectations you have about a tenant, it is useful, and beyond that, pleasant, to think about whom you would like to have as a tenant. Would you like to have children around? Would you like to have someone who shares your religious beliefs? Would you like to have someone who likes gardening and can help keep up your garden? Do you want to have a neighbor who plays bridge? Do you want a freshly scrubbed, young college student who is excruciatingly polite?

Knowing whom you would like to have as a tenant is important, because there are ways to advertise that make it more likely you'll get such a person. If you want a polite college student, putting notices on the bulletin boards of a polite college is a good way to start. If you want someone who shares your religious beliefs, put a notice in the bulletin of your church or synagogue. Even if you are going to use a real estate agent, it will be helpful in your discussion if you have thought ahead of time about the kind of person you want.

No matter how you are going to advertise the apartment, it is useful to write down a basic description of what you are offering. You can use it in discussing the apartment with friends, as a guide when placing a classified ad, and as a notice for bulletin boards. Doreen Bierbrier makes the point that, in advertising, it is also useful to include information designed to save you time. You don't want to get a large number of calls from college students if you don't want college students. The following is a checklist of information your ad should include:

- Size of apartment, including number of bedrooms and whether living room, dining room, and kitchen are separate from each other.
- Fact that it is in a single-family home.
- Where located in home, if basement or attic apartment.
- Amount of rent, and whether utilities are included.
- Preferred age of tenants.
- Number of tenants permitted and whether or not children and pets are permitted.

- Location relative to shopping, public transportation, colleges, or large employers.
- Availability of parking, particularly in urban areas.
- Available appliances, such as washer, dryer, and air conditioning.
- Phone number to call, and appropriate times to call.
- Any particular features of the apartment, such as private entrance or yard area.
- People you don't want—college students, smokers, etc.

If you have any doubts about the need for making up such an advertisement before you start to talk to people or call the classifieds, you won't after you call the classifieds. Few experiences are more humiliating than talking to the classified section of a newspaper without being prepared.

On the other hand, so long as you know what you want to say, most people who take classifieds over the phone are very helpful in making sure the ad is clear and that it is as short and therefore as inexpensive as possible.

If you are going to use bulletin boards, remember to write your phone number across the bottom or side as many times as you can, and then cut slits between the numbers with a pair of scissors. As anybody who loves reading bulletin boards will tell you, this gives interested people a slip to tear off easily with your phone number on it. Development of this technique has been a major advance in bulletin board technology.

Also, in making up your ad, if you want to shorten it for use on a bulletin board or in the classifieds, look at the classifieds themselves as a guide. They will have standard local abbreviations for things, such as AC for air conditioning. Also, as mentioned earlier in the chapter on finances, they will be a good guide to how much rent is being charged for similar apartments. Finally, if you want to select tenants who are old, or who are of one sex or the other, the classifieds will generally not let you advertise that preference.

Choosing Where to Advertise

There are four main choices in advertising for tenants, as mentioned before. You can go through a real estate agent for a fee, you can use the classifieds, you can use bulletin boards, and you can use newsletters. As noted earlier, the bulletin boards and the newsletters let you be very selective about who gets your message. They are also cheaper. Their drawback is that they reach fewer people.

If you want to reach people from your religious community or from a local college, you should clearly go the bulletin board or newsletter route. If you like sports, try a tennis or racquetball club bulletin board. It may be slower, but that may not be as important to you as getting the tenant with the exact background you want. A little creativity can go a long way in this situation. Think of what you like, and what kind of person you like, and where that kind of person is likely to be found.

The classifieds may bring you more response sooner, and if you have just finished installing the apartment and have to make payments on a loan to the bank, you will want the rent coming in right away.

Perhaps the most important thing to remember about renting your apartment is that the process may be less mechanical than you expect. Most people are used to having things happen in a straightforward way. You turn the key in your car and it starts. There are more surprises in renting an apartment. An ad in the classifieds may have the phone ringing off the hook one week and produce only two phone calls the next. If you don't get much initial response when you advertise, however you choose to do it, accept your worry as to be expected, and don't take it too seriously. Think about reasons why you might not be getting the right response, but don't assume immediately that something is wrong. Renting an apartment is not as straightforward as starting a car. It's more like threading a needle: It may take a few tries, and being overanxious is pretty much a waste of time.

Interviewing Techniques

Whether you are talking to tenants on the phone or showing them the apartment, there are a few practical things to remember. Most of these suggestions are drawn from Doreen Bierbrier's book.

First, start on neutral ground by describing the apartment, good points and bad. Take your time. It puts the potential tenant at ease. Also, being straightforward about the bad points will generally make people trust you.

Second, be suspicious of anyone who is in a great hurry. People who are in a desperate hurry often are having trouble managing their own lives and, in the absence of a good, clearly stated explanation, may not be the most stable tenants.

Third, don't be afraid to say no, or at least, "We promised to let someone else look at it before we rented it. Can we call you back tomorrow?" Then call back tomorrow and say no. Remember, in a very practical sense you are not in this to be nice to people. You want someone living close to you whom it will be a pleasure to have as a neighbor. It will take a large rental income to make up for having a disagreeable neighbor. If you don't like somebody, say no, and say it in a way, perhaps over the telephone, that doesn't involve you in a long explanation of a personality conflict. If you are saying no over the telephone, you can always find a polite excuse to get off the phone, such as "I've got something burning in the oven."

Getting Assistance from a Friend

As discussed earlier, the mere idea of raising some of the questions listed above is probably enough to make many people slam the door on the whole idea of installing an accessory apartment. However, there is strength in numbers. Ask a friend or relative to be with you when you interview prospective tenants. The best reason for doing this is because it makes it more fun. After the prospective tenants leave, you can have a good gossip about what they are like.

Most of us still have grade-school scoldings about the evils of gossip in our heads, but this case is different. Gossip here is not only fun, it's a good practice. As both a landlord and a close neighbor, it will be very important to find someone you like as a tenant. Often it will help you a great deal to be able to talk over the personality of prospective tenants with someone else. The result may not always be perfect. You may not always get tenants who will also be great friends. But you will greatly improve your chances of squeezing a lemon of a tenant out of the running before he or she puckers up your life.

The second reason for having someone else with you when you do interviews, or even having someone else receive initial phone calls from prospective tenants, is more obvious. If you are nervous about asking the important questions, pick someone to help you who will not be.

Checking References

Once you have a person or persons you think will be good tenants, check their references. Checking references is a nuisance, and generally you learn little, which is good. It's the times you do learn something that you should worry about. All you need is one call that makes you gasp with relief at not having accepted a tenant, and you will become a firm believer in checking references.

This of course assumes that you have gotten references when you interviewed the prospective tenants. It is admittedly impossible to do all the things that you ought to do, but getting references is one thing you should do. You should get references of prior landlords if at all possible.

When you call up references, pay particular attention to what people might be saying. Suddenly being in the position of having practical power, such as giving information that will determine whether or not someone gets an apartment, tends to make people much more cautious. Often you have to listen for hints. If the reference says, "Well, she was occasionally a little slow with the rent," follow up and find out exactly how slow. If the reference says, "He occasionally came home a little tipsy," find out how occasionally and how tipsy.

Finally, Doreen Bierbrier makes a very good point. If you are going to call only one reference, don't call the landlord whose apartment the tenant is just leaving. Call the prior landlord. Once in a while a tenant's current landlord will give you a bum steer because the tenant isn't fit to live in a doghouse, and the landlord is only too eager to get the tenant out of his or her apartment and into yours.

Fair Housing Laws

Laws prohibiting discrimination in housing do not force homeowners with accessory apartments to rent to someone they do not want to rent to. The Civil Rights Act of 1968, which forbids discrimination in housing, does not apply to buildings of four apartments or less, "if the owner actually maintains and occupies one of such living quarters as his residence."

In other words, if you are renting an accessory apartment in a home you live in, you cannot be accused of racial discrimination under federal law.

There are also state and local laws prohibiting discrimination based on race. Almost universally, however, they also do not apply to rental of an accessory apartment in a home occupied by the homeowner.

There are also laws prohibiting discrimination based on age, sex, sexual preference, and presence of children in the household. These laws, which exist at the federal, state, and local levels, again almost universally exempt a resident homeowner renting an accessory apartment. If you are nervous about them, or about being threatened with discrimination on any grounds, the best thing to do is call the appropriate state or local agency and ask how the laws apply to your situation. You can also call the nearest regional office of the U.S. Department of Housing and Urban Development. Usually, however, the local agency, which will typically be a human rights or equal opportunity commission, will be able to explain all the applicable laws. They will also be willing to send you additional information.

One additional point should be made. A famous black leader once stated that there is nothing more middle class than a middle-class black. He was making specific the generally accepted principle that many individuals from groups that have been subjected to stereotyping and prejudice spend a great deal of energy trying to overcome those attitudes in the way they lead their individual lives. Typically, therefore, they make great tenants. What it comes down to is that if you discriminate on any of the usual grounds you will probably be passing up many of the best tenants.

It makes a great deal more sense just to treat people as individuals. Do you like them or don't you? Do they make you feel at ease? Have they got a stable source of income to pay the rent? There are good tenants and there are bad tenants. The way to avoid the bad ones, and there are not that many, is to judge people individually, not to discriminate.

Insurance

You should think about insurance in two ways. First, is your house covered by your homeowner's insurance once you have a tenant in it? The only way to answer that question is to call your insurance agent. Individual companies vary, but in most cases they have not had problems with tenants in accessory apartments. Their reasoning, according to one major company, is that although there is some added risk since there are more people in the house, the added people also mean added protection against such things as fire or other damage when the homeowner is away. As mentioned earlier, you should talk to your insurance agent in any case about increasing insurance to cover the value you have added to the house with the accessory apartment.

In addition, you should think about whether you want your tenant to have insurance. Your insurance will not typically cover the tenant's possessions. In addition, you may want your tenant to have insurance so that you can be repaid if the tenant causes damage that is not covered by your own insurance policy. It would be very wise to require the tenant to take out insurance if, for example, your own insurance agent informed you that your policy covered any damage to your home except that caused by a tenant.

Leases

Most leases are designed on the "Good fences make good neighbors" principle. With human beings being what they are, it takes pretty good fences to make them into good neighbors. As a result, most standard leases get pretty complex. Don't be overwhelmed by feeling you should know every last detail of a standard lease form.

You can get a lease form from most local stationery stores. Call first to make sure they have them available. Once you get a lease form, read it over. If you are going to be careful, you should probably call your local government's landlord and tenant relations office or its closest equivalent, which may be a housing office of some kind. Tell them what form you have picked up and check that it is consistent with state and local laws on rental housing.

You may get an acute case of boredom from reading the lease, but leases certainly are more interesting than usual if you're a potential landlord. They usually make you feel well protected.

A Sample Lease

A sample lease agreement from the Montgomery County, Maryland, Office of Landlord and Tenant Affairs is included here for reference. Note that it is not specifically for accessory apartments but for condominium and cooperative rentals, which in some ways are very similar. Note also that the lease is only a sample. It was developed to illustrate the kinds of things tenants and landlords should look for in a lease. It also has the advantage of being written in plain English.

The sample lease is marked "Void—Not Negotiable" because the county does not want the legal responsibility that apparently comes with preparing a standard form. In any case, laws that affect the provisions in a lease vary from community to community and state to state. However, the sample lease is a valuable, easy-to-read checklist for things that you may want to have in your lease.

Some of the items in the lease deserve comment because of the way they apply to accessory apartments. Each item that needs additional comment is noted by a *. The comments are listed by item following the lease.

SAMPLE LEASE

MULTI-FAMILY RESIDENTIAL LEASE AGREEMENT FOR CONDOMINIUM AND COOPERATIVE RENTALS MONTGOMERY COUNTY, MARYLAND

DATE OF, PARTIES TO, CONTRACT

1. This Rental Contract is made and executed this _____ day of _____, 19 _____, by and between _____ and _____, hereinafter called "Tenant," _____ hereinafter called "Cosigner" and _____ _____ hereinafter called "Landlord."

PREMISES, INITIAL TERM, RENT

2. Landlord rents to Tenant for residential purposes only, the premises known as Apartment Number _____, _____, _____ located in Montgomery County, Maryland, for the term of _____ month(s) commencing on the _____ day of _____, 19 ___, and fully ending at midnight on the _____ day of _____, 19 ___, for the total rental of _____ Dollars and _____ Cents ($), payable in equal, consecutive monthly installments of _____ Dollars and _____ Cents ($), for the second twelve months, representing an increase of ___% over the monthly rent charged during the first year, in order to offset projected increased operating expenses. Each payment is due without diminution, deduction or demand in full accord with Covenants 11 and 12, on or before the close of business, on the FIRST day of each month during the term or any subsequent renewal, at the business office of Landlord, _____ _____, or at such other place Landlord shall from time to time designate.

193

**DELIVERY DATE
PRO RATA RENT**

3.   Tenant shall take possession of the premises on the _____ day of _____ 19 ___, and shall pay the sum of _____ Dollars and _____ Cents ($) from that date through _____. Thereafter, rent shall be paid in accordance with Covenants 2 and 9.

*UTILITIES

4.   Tenant agrees to promptly pay, in addition to the rent, the following utilities (unless struck and initialled by Landlord and Tenant, in which case the utilities struck shall be provided by the Landlord and included in the rent payment): heat, gas, electricity and water.

_____ [Tenant(s)]

_____ [Landlord]

Landlord may require Tenant to demonstrate proof of payment at any time during tenancy.

***AUTHORIZED
OCCUPANTS**

5.   a. Enumerated. In addition to Tenant(s) listed in Covenant 1, the following persons and no others, except afterborn children, are authorized by Landlord to reside within the leased premises: _____. No other persons may reside in the premises without first obtaining Landlord's written consent.

b. Limitation on number. To help insure enjoyable and tranquil living conditions at the rental facility, Landlord reserves the right to uniformly and impartially regulate the maximum number of occupants permitted to reside within this size dwelling unit, which policy may be more stringent than minimum overcrowding requirements specified in Chapter 26, Montgomery County Code. Tenant acknowledges that the maximum number of persons permitted to reside within this dwelling unit shall not exceed _____ (   ) persons. Should more than the maximum number be found to reside in the dwelling unit, Landlord may bring court action for repossession of the premises based upon Tenant breach of this Covenant.

c. Guests. Persons visiting Tenant may not reside at the premises for more than two weeks in aggregate during any calendar year, unless written permission is first secured from Landlord. Tenant's guests and visitors shall abide by all applicable covenants and rules herein contained, so that a breach by a guest or visitor shall be treated as a breach by Tenant himself.

*COSIGNER

6. A Cosigner for Tenant to this Agreement shall act solely as surety or guarantor, agreeing to be held liable for any and all unmet financial responsibilities incurred by Tenant to the detriment of Landlord in connection with this Agreement to include, but not limited to Tenant's obligation to pay rent, late fees, damage due to breach of lease, and any other costs to Landlord resulting from Tenant acts or negligence which produce damage to the premises or any part of the rental facility. Cosigner may not occupy the premises and shall not be considered a tenant without Landlord's prior written consent.

RENTAL APPLICATION

7. a. Part of agreement. Tenant's completed Rental Application is made part of this Agreement; a copy is affixed to all copies of this Lease.

b. Truth a condition. Statements and representations made by Tenant in applying for occupancy of premises at the rental facility induced Landlord to enter into this Agreement, and if any are found to be materially misleading, incorrect or untrue, Landlord shall be entitled to terminate this Agreement by operation of law and without a showing that Landlord was actually injured by the misrepresentation(s) or misleading statement(s). Each Tenant listed above expressly warrants that he is of legal age to enter into this Agreement, such warranty being made to induce Landlord to execute this Agreement and lease the premises listed in Covenant 2.

JOINT AND SEVERAL LIABILITY

8.   a. Generally. Each tenant listed above shall be jointly and severally responsible to landlord for full performance under each and every covenant and condition of this Lease Agreement and for compliance with applicable law.

b. Notices. Any written notice regarding tenancy given by one Tenant to Landlord or by Landlord to one Tenant shall affect and apply, with equal force, to all Tenants, authorized occupants and, if applicable, Cosigner and Subtenant.

RENT INCREASES

9.   a. Frequency and amount. After the initial term of this Agreement, Landlord May, from time to time and to the maximum amount permitted by law, increase rent for the demised dwelling unit.

b. Notice. Sixty (60) days' prior written notice of a rent increase shall be mailed to Tenant; it shall also expressly serve as two (2) full months notice to quit and vacate the premises in the event Tenant does not agree to pay the rent increase. Landlord shall not accept rent payment less than that called for by the rent increase notice; and in the event Tenant remains in possession on the date the rent increase is to be effective, failing to pay the increased rent and thereby holding over beyond the period specified in the quit and vacate notice, Landlord may immediately file suit to evict Tenant.

c. Acceptance. Tenant shall express acceptance of Landlord's offer to increase rent by timely payment, in full, of the new rent as specified in the rent increase notice, in which event the notice to quit shall be void.

FORM OF PAYMENTS

10.   All rent installments shall be made by check only addressed to _____

and mailed to Landlord's business office as aforementioned, unless notified otherwise. Landlord has the right to require any and all rent installments be paid by cash or money order; written receipts shall be provided for all cash and money orders paid by Tenant to Landlord for rent, security or otherwise. Deposits, fees, bills and other costs to Landlord resulting from Tenant breach of Lease, or Tenant acts or negligence, shall be treated and considered as additional rent due and owing, subject to all provisions contained in this Agreement regarding rent payment. Partial payment of any charge against Tenant arising from this Lease of applicable law shall not relieve Tenant of the obligation to make full and timely payment to Landlord, unless written notice is secured from Landlord honoring partial payment as full settlement of the particular debt or financial responsibility.

*LATE FEES

11. If Landlord shall fail to receive an installment or part of rent within ten (10) days after it is due, Tenant shall pay Landlord without demand, in addition to the rent, a late charge of five percent (5%) of the rent due for the rental period for which rent is delinquent. Such payment is not a waiver of the fact that rent is due on the FIRST of the month. This Covenant does not waive or limit Landlord's right to institute legal proceedings for rent, additional forms of rent listed in Covenant 10, other damages and/or repossession of the premises.

SECURITY DEPOSIT

12. a. Handled in accordance with law. Tenant shall give Landlord a security deposit of _____ Dollars ($), receipt for which is hereby given Tenant. It shall be held by Landlord during tenancy as security for full or partial payment of unpaid rent; damage due to breach of Lease; or damage to the leased premises in excess of ordinary wear and tear caused by Tenant, his family, agent,

employee, visitor or guest. Within thirty (30) days after receipt of the security deposit, Landlord shall deposit it in an escrow account devoted exclusively to security deposits in a banking or savings institution, as required by law. Landlord shall, within thirty (30) days after the termination of tenancy, present by first-class mail to the last known address of Tenant a written list of damages to the premises itemizing charges assessed against Tenant, together with a statement of the cost actually incurred. Within forty-five (45) days after the termination of tenancy, Landlord shall mail to the last known address of Tenant the security deposit plus four percent (4%) per year simple interest accruing at six-month intervals, less any damages rightfully withheld. Refer also to Covenants 13.b. and e.

b. Notices. Tenancy (Tenant's right to occupy the premises and Tenant's obligations under this Lease) shall not end merely because Tenant ceases to occupy the premises. Notices shall be forwarded to Tenant based upon termination of tenancy, not termination of actual occupancy, though the two may coincide.

c. No deduction by Tenant. Tenant shall not deduct his last or any month's rent or any charge from the security deposit: Landlord may file suit to recover any such rent deficiency or unpaid debt.

CONDITION OF PREMISES

13. a. Delivered in compliance with law. Landlord covenants that the leased premises are delivered in a clean, safe and sanitary condition, free of rodents and vermin and in complete compliance with applicable law. Tenant acknowledges he has been given an opportunity to examine the premises, that he has examined the premises and found the dwelling unit in satisfactory condition. All smoke detectors required by the Montgomery County Code,

Section 26-21, are installed and in proper working condition.

b. List of existing damages. Within fifteen (15) days of occupancy, Tenant has the option of requesting of Landlord, in writing, a list of all existing damages to the premises. Tenant acknowledges he had been supplied a form, which is attached to all copies of the Lease, upon which to enumerate any existing damages. Upon Landlord's receipt of this form within fifteen (15) days of Tenant's occupancy, Landlord shall promptly inspect the dwelling unit to confirm or deny the existence of damages claimed to exist prior to Tenant's occupancy; a copy of the inspection report shall thereafter be filed with Tenant.

c. Landlord's responsibility for maintenance of premises. Montgomery County Code Chapter 8, "Buildings"; Chapter 22, "Fire Prevention"; Chapter 26, "Housing Standards"; and Chapter 59, "Zoning," are incorporated by reference into this Agreement as an express warranty of habitability and covenant to repair. Under no circumstances is Tenant to alter, repair, decorate or physically attach Tenant property to the premises, unless Landlord's written permission is obtained. (A reasonable number of picture hangers is permitted.)

d. Surrender. Tenant shall leave the premises in a broom-clean condition, free of trash and debris, and shall not paint marks; plaster holes, crevices or cracks; or embark on any repair of the premises without Landlord's prior written consent. Tenant shall be charged in accordance with Covenants 10, 12.a., 14.a. and b.

e. Tenant's right to be present at inspection of premises. Tenant has the right to be present at the time of Landlord's inspection of the premises for damages, if Tenant notifies Landlord by certified mail of his intention to move, the date of moving and his new address.

The notice to be furnished by Tenant to Landlord shall be mailed at least fifteen (15) days prior to the date of moving. Upon receipt of the notice, Landlord shall notify Tenant by certified mail of the time and date when the premises are to be inspected. The date of inspection shall, at the discretion of Landlord, occur within five (5) days before or five (5) days after the date of moving designated in Tenant's notice.

DAMAGES TO PREMISES

14.   a. Duty to report. Tenant shall promptly report to Landlord any damage to, or defect found within, the dwelling unit so that Landlord may effect repairs diligently. When failure of Tenant to so report the known existence of damages or defects within his dwelling unit causes injury or damage to any part of the rental facility or any person, Tenant shall be liable for resulting damages or injuries.

b. Tenant caused. When acts or omissions of Tenant, his family, visitors, guests or employees, whether negligent, reckless or intentional, cause damage to any part of the rental facility or to Landlord's employees, Tenant shall promptly pay expenses incurred by Landlord to correct such damages upon presentation of a bill itemizing the costs involved. That amount shall be considered additional rent due on the FIRST of the month following Tenant's receipt of the bill. Whether claimed by Landlord or Tenant, all charges for repair of damages to the premises shall be itemized and, upon written request, substantiated. Tenant shall not make repairs to the premises without Landlord's written permission.

c. Landlord caused. Landlord shall be under no liability to Tenant due to any damages to or inconvenience experienced by Tenant of whatever nature, unless caused by the negligent acts of Landlord or Landlord's violation of any law, in which case Tenant shall be reimbursed for damages so sustained.

d. Renter's insurance. Tenant is strongly urged to obtain an insurance policy so that Tenant may be protected against damages to his property and person which may take place in or about the dwelling unit, but which occur without the negligence of Landlord.

*SUBLET

15.   Tenant shall not sublet, rent or assign this Lease, transfer possession of the premises or any portion thereof to any other person without obtaining prior written consent of Landlord. Landlord's permission to sublet shall not be unreasonably withheld; provided that no legal documents and rules and regulations of the condominium and/or cooperative, whichever applicable, prohibits subleasing; and the prospective subtenant satisfies established standards set forth by Landlord for all prospective tenants of the rental facility, including, but not limited to, a credit check, rental and employment references and Tenant's payment of $ _____ reasonable service charge defraying Landlord's expenses incidental to processing the application for subtenancy. The above charge shall also apply in the event of assignment or other transfer of this Lease. In the case of subletting, Tenant may be held liable for any breach of this Agreement by Subtenant. Tenant may only sublet during the initial term of this Lease.

*CANCELLATION
BY TENANT
DURING
INITIAL TERM

16.   a. Reasonable cause beyond Tenant control. The initial term of this Lease may be terminated upon change of employment from the Washington metropolitan area, death of major wage earner, unemployment or for other reasonable cause beyond Tenant control. Tenant shall provide Landlord with written proof of such involuntary change of employment more than twenty-five (25) miles from the Washington area (for example, signed military orders or transfer papers signed by employer). If other

reasonable cause beyond Tenant's control is claimed, Tenant shall specify the specific causes in writing to Landlord, who may verify and accept or reject such claims, depending upon the particular circumstances. In the event of termination under this Covenant, Tenant shall pay a termination charge equivalent to one (1) month's rent (at the rate in effect as of termination) or actual damages sustained by Landlord, whichever is the lesser amount; the termination charge to be in addition to rent due and owing through said termination date, rent due during the notice period, and the security deposit already posted. The one-month's rent termination charge shall be made in advance with the Tenant's notice to vacate and rent for the notice period. A refund to Tenant shall be made if actual damages are less than the termination fee.

b. Reason within Tenant control (for example, House purchase, voluntary job change, marriage). One (1) full month's written notice to quit and vacate—to run from the first of the month to the last day of the same month—shall be given to Landlord. Tenant shall be responsible for rent payment during that period. Furthermore, Tenant shall be responsible for reasonable advertising and redecoration expenses, lost rent, and other costs incurred by Landlord as a result of Tenant's premature termination of this Agreement. Landlord is not obligated to provide Tenant with notice that the dwelling unit has been rerented. Upon rerental, Tenant may be held secondarily liable for default(s) by subsequent Tenant(s) in the payment of rent during the balance of the initial term of this Lease. Landlord is under no obligation to rent Tenant's vacant dwelling unit before any other vacant dwelling unit at the rental facility.

c. Surrender. In addition to 13.d., Tenant shall surrender possession to Landlord upon the elapse of Tenant's notice to vacate. Failure to vacate may result in the filing of court action to evict. Tenant may also be held accountable for actual damages caused by the holding over and for consequential damages due to an incoming tenant's inability to enter because of Tenant's unlawful occupancy. Abandoned Tenant property shall, at Landlord's option, become Landlord's property, or Landlord may dispose of it without liability to Tenant or the owner of property left within the dwelling unit. Prior to vacating, Tenant shall surrender all keys issued by Landlord and all duplicates of same; failure to do so shall be sufficient cause for Landlord to replace locks and keys for the dwelling unit at the Tenant's expense.

*CANCELLATION
BY LANDLORD
DURING
INITIAL TERM

17. If Tenant, his guests, visitors, employees, family or invitees display objectionable conduct or otherwise materially breach this Lease, Landlord shall issue Tenant a one (1) month notice to vacate the premises (or any shorter period permitted by law). Failure to vacate will activate Covenant 16.c.

CANCELLATION
AT END OF
INITIAL TERM

18. Either Landlord or Tenant may terminate this Lease as of the end of the initial term by providing the other party with at least one (1) full month's prior written notice to vacate—to run from the first of the month to the last day of the same month. No reason need be stated in the notice by the issuing party. Failure to vacate in accordance with the notice to vacate will activate Covenant 16.c.

MONTH-TO-MONTH
TENANCY

19. a. Creation. If this Lease has not been lawfully cancelled during or at the end of the initial term (as provided in Covenants 16, 17 or 18), a month-to-month, automatically renewable tenancy shall be created. All other provisions of this Lease shall remain in force.

b. Termination by Landlord. The month-to-month tenancy may be terminated upon tenant's receipt of at least two (2) full months' notice to vacate the premises, which notice shall be received before the first of the month and shall be effective through the last day of the second month (corresponding with two (2) rent payment intervals). Tenant shall be responsible for rent payment during the notice period. The reason for termination need not be specified in the notice to vacate. Landlord shall be held harmless from all charges of libel related to Tenant's requesting Landlord's reason for terminating this Agreement. Covenant 16.c. also fully applies.

    c. Termination by Tenant. The month-to-month tenancy may be terminated upon Landlord's receipt of at least one (1) month's notice to vacate to be received by Landlord before the first of the month and to extend through the last day of the same month. Tenant shall be responsible for rent during the notice period. No reason for termination need be specified in the notice. Covenant 16.c. applies.

EVICTION HELP

20.   In the event of eviction by judicial process, Tenant has the right to request, through the Office of Landlord-Tenant Affairs, general information and assistance regarding evictions and moving services and storage accommodations, provided such services are not otherwise available to Tenant. This request may be made prior to or immediately following the entry of judgment for nonpayment of rent. Moving and storage services shall be at Tenant's expense or, if such assistance is available, with financial assistance from the County.

*LANDLORD ACCESS

21.   a. When permitted. Landlord shall have access to the demised premises
    1)   In any emergency;
    2)   After due notice, when Landlord has good cause to believe Tenant may have damaged the premises, breached this Agree-

ment or violated Montgomery County Code Chapter 29, "Landlord–Tenant Relations";

3) After due notice, at all reasonable times for the purpose of making such repairs or alterations or taking such action as necessary to effect compliance with the provisions of Montgomery County Code, Chapter 26, "Housing Standards," or any lawful order issued pursuant to the provisions of Chapter 26;

4) During normal business hours, after due notice from Landlord and without objection from Tenant, for the purpose of making necessary repairs, decorations, alterations, improvements or supplying services—Tenant's service request shall be interpreted as permission to enter during normal business hours unless Landlord is notified otherwise by Tenant; and

5) During normal business hours including weekends, after due notice from Landlord and without objection from Tenant, for the purpose of exhibiting the dwelling unit to prospective purchasers, mortgagees or tenants.

b. Inability to enter. Tenant shall be held responsible for any damages caused by Landlord's inability to gain access to the dwelling unit to effect repair or to remedy an emergency, where such inability is caused by Tenant in violation of this Lease.

TENANT OBLIGATIONS

22. Tenant is responsible for keeping the premises which he occupies and uses as clean, sanitary and safe as the conditions of the premises permit; disposing from his dwelling unit all rubbish, garbage and other organic or flammable waste in a clean and sanitary manner; keeping all plumbing fixtures as clean and sanitary as their condition permits; and for proper use and operation of all electrical and

plumbing fixtures. Tenant must not permit any person on the premises with his permission to willfully or wantonly destroy, deface, damage, impair or remove any part of the structure of the dwelling unit or its facilities, equipment or appurtenances, nor shall Tenant himself do any such thing. Tenant will not use or allow any part of the dwelling unit to be used for any disorderly or unlawful purpose, nor will he do anything on or about the premises or rental facility that causes injury, damage, hurt, inconvenience, annoyance or discomfort to any employee of Landlord or other tenant at the rental facility. Tenant will conform to the rules and regulations now in effect. Rules hereafter made by Landlord, which are consented to in writing by Tenant, shall also be binding. A copy of existing Rules is attached to and made part of this Lease.

FIRE, UNAVOIDABLE ACCIDENT

23.   If the premises are damaged by fire, rain, wind or other cause beyond the control of Landlord, unless the same shall occur for any reason for which Tenant is responsible, the premises shall be repaired within a reasonable time at the expense of Landlord; and in case the damage is so extensive as to render the premises untenantable, the rent shall cease until the premises are repaired. If the premises are totally destroyed without fault of Tenant, rent shall be paid up to the time of destruction, and this Lease shall come to an end.

LICENSE

24.   A copy of the license to operate this rental facility in Montgomery County, Maryland, may be inspected by Tenant during normal business hours at _____.

COMPROMISE NON-ENFORCE-MENT

25.   If a court proceeding for repossession or non-payment of rent shall be commenced and a settlement or compromise effected either before or after judgment whereby Tenant shall be permitted to retain possession of the prem-

ises, such proceeding or compromise shall not constitute a waiver of any condition or covenant contained herein or of any subsequent breach of this Agreement. Landlord's failure to enforce a provision of this Agreement will not operate to permit a similar or subsequent breach of any provision of this Agreement by this or any tenant at the rental facility.

★UTILITY CONVERSION

26. As of the date of this Lease, Landlord ___ does ___ does not (check one) intend to convert the responsibility for payment of any utilities now being provided by the Landlord for the premises to direct payment by Tenant. Notice is hereby given to Tenant by Landlord that Landlord reserves the right to convert the responsibility for payment of any of such utilities to Tenant at any time whether during the initial term of this Lease or otherwise upon the following conditions:

a. *Notice:* Tenant shall receive written notice at least two (2) months prior to the effective date of the conversion; the notice will be an offer to reduce the Tenant's rent in an amount commensurate with the monthly average of actual utility consumption experienced by the Landlord during the previous twenty-four (24) months.

b. *Date of transfer of payment:* Transfer of financial responsibility for payment of any utilities converted to direct payment by the Lessee shall occur at the commencement of a rent payment cycle, namely on the first day of a month.

c. *Access:* Landlord, upon the giving of appropriate notice as called for by subsections (a) and (c) of this Covenant, shall have the right to enter Tenant's premises during normal business hours providing Tenant is given two (2) days' advance notice in writing of the date and time of such proposed entry and Tenant has no reasonable objection thereto.

d. *Submetering:* Any utility submetering

shall be accomplished in accordance with law and the regulations promulgated by the Maryland Public Service Commission.

GENDER, NUMBER, SEVERABILITY

27.   Within the provisions of this Agreement, feminine or neuter pronouns shall be substituted for those of masculine form, and the plural shall be substituted for the singular number any place in which the context may require such substitution. If any provision, clause, sentence, section or part of this Lease is held illegal, the remaining provisions, clauses, sentences or sections shall not be affected or impaired. To the extent that a portion of this Agreement may be invalid unless certain words or phrases are struck, such words and phrases shall be deemed to be struck, and the remainder of the provisions and other portions of this Agreement shall remain in full force and effect.

ENTIRE AGREEMENT

28.   This document contains the final and entire Agreement between the parties hereto, and no party shall be bound by any term, condition or representation, oral or written, not set forth or provided herein. The conditions, covenants and Rules contained in this Lease may be legally enforced by the parties of this Agreement, their heirs, successors and assigns, respectively. Nothing shall prevent modification of the terms of this Lease by mutual agreement through the execution of a written Addendum affixed to all copies of this Lease.

I agree to abide by all the terms of this Agreement:

Landlord _____   Date _____

Witness _____   Date _____

Tenant _____   Date _____

Witness _____   Date _____

Tenant _____ Date _____

Witness _____ Date _____

Cosigner _____ Date _____

Witness _____ Date _____

RULES

*1. LAUNDRY, STORAGE ROOMS. In the event Landlord sets apart in the rental facility a laundry or storage room for the convenience of Tenant, Tenant may, at his own risk, use such facilities. Employees of Landlord are prohibited as such from in any way storing, moving or handling Tenant's articles in or from the laundry or storage room, and if any such employee at the request of Tenant takes part in storing, handling, opening or moving anything in, for or from such laundry or storage room, he shall be doing so as agent of Tenant, not Landlord.

2. NO COMBUSTIBLES. Tenant will not allow any gasoline or other combustible materials to be kept in or about the leased premises, or permit or do anything which would increase the rate of fire insurance upon the rental facility.

*3. PARKING. If automobile parking space is provided by Landlord for convenience of Tenant, it will not be used for the parking or storage of boats, trucks, trailers, commercial or recreational vehicles, or for the storage of automobiles. Tenant agrees to obey all posted signs and space markings. Landlord assumes no responsibility or liability whatever for loss or damage to any automobile while parked on said space, except as provided by law. Tenant shall not wash or make repairs to automobiles at any place on or about the rental facility. Parked automobiles shall, at all times, display current tags and be in operating condition; otherwise, the automobiles will, five (5) days after tagging, be towed away at Tenant's expense without further notice.

4. CARPETING. To lessen noise caused or occasioned by walking on the floors of the leased premises, Tenant agrees to install a reasonable amount of carpeting to cover not less than ___% of the floor area, excluding the kitchen, bathroom(s) and closets.

5. CONTRIVANCES. Tenant shall place no additional locks or locking devices upon any doors or windows in, on or about the leased premises without first securing Landlord's permission in writing. No per-

sonal property, except a reasonable number of picture hangers, shall be attached to the dwelling unit without obtaining prior written approval from Landlord. Tenant shall not install any exterior wiring or aerial for television or radio on roof or exterior of building, and Tenant shall not install or place in the leased premises any washing machines, home laundry device or similar equipment without written Landlord consent.

*6.   PETS. Tenant shall not keep or maintain, or allow a visitor to bring onto any part of the rental facility, any dog, cat, bird or other pet animal, whether wild or domestic, without Landlord's written consent.

7.   SMOKE DETECTORS. Tenant shall be responsible for replacement of any batteries for, and shall report promptly to Landlord any defective operation of, the smoke detector mechanism. Tenant shall also periodically test batteries to insure that the smoke detector is operating properly.

8.   LIGHT BULBS. Landlord shall furnish electric light bulbs of proper wattage in fixtures installed by Landlord at the time Tenant takes possession of the leased premises, but not thereafter.

9.   ARTICLES LEFT IN COMMON AREAS. Tenant shall not leave personal property in any common area in the rental facility.

I agree to abide by these Rules which form a part of the Lease:

Landlord _____ Date _____

Witness _____ Date _____

Tenant _____ Date _____

Witness _____ Date _____

Tenant _____ Date _____

Witness _____ Date _____

Cosigner _____ Date _____

Witness _____ Date _____

Items in the Lease That Need Additional Discussion

Utilities: In many accessory apartments, the utilities are not separated from those of the homeowner. In others, only one utility, such as the electricity or the heat, is separate. Since this can give rise to confusion, a provision discussing who is responsible for utilities is almost always necessary.

Authorized Occupants: The term "afterborn children" means children born after the lease is signed.

Guests: Since guests may mean a particular inconvenience for the owner of an accessory apartment, either through noise, parking, children in the yard, or various other problems, this is a particularly useful provision for owners of accessory apartments. You can always tell the tenant verbally that you are willing to permit a guest or two for a longer time under specific conditions and by prior arrangement.

Cosigner: This is probably not a very useful provision for homeowners with accessory apartments. Cosigners often cost too much to track down, particularly if they are not only from out of town but also out of state. An alternative means of protecting yourself is to charge a higher security deposit, such as two months' rent, so long as doing so is not prohibited by state law. However, this may put off some potential tenants.

Late Fees: There may be state and local laws that govern what late fees you can charge.

Sublet: For most homeowners, it is preferable not to permit subleases, simply to ensure that they have greater control over who will live in their apartment. Instead, the landlord should have a penalty for early termination, as discussed in the next section.

Cancellation by Tenant During Initial Term: If you intend to travel much, this is an important provision. You do not want to have to come home from a trip in order to find a new tenant. Your costs in doing so may exceed the termination charge. Accordingly, you may want to increase the termination . charge beyond that suggested by this lease, or make specific arrangements with your tenant before each extended trip that specify an appropriate termination charge. The same issues are raised by the Month-to-Month Tenancy provision that is further on in the sample lease. However, you should know that in some states termination charges may be legally limited.

Cancellation by Landlord During Initial Term: This provision, or a similar one, is an essential provision for a homeowner with an accessory apartment to have. You want it to be as strong as possible so that in the event you do end up with an undesirable tenant, you can do something about it as soon as possible.

Landlord Access: This is a critical issue for accessory apartment owners who may need to get in the apartment because utility systems are not separated or for a variety of other reasons. In particular, the kind of prior notice that the homeowner should give the tenant needs to be well defined. It is probably not adequately defined in this lease for the purposes of an accessory apartment.

Utility Conversion: This is a particularly useful provision for a homeowner to include in a list if the homeowner has any doubts about the way utilities are currently separated.

Laundry, Storage Rooms: If there are a washer and dryer tenants can use, you may want to set times on when they are available, so that you don't wake at 2 a.m. to the thumping and whirling of a dryer.

Parking: This is another particularly useful rule for accessory apartment owners. Homeowners may want to incorporate in it rules about washing cars.

Pets: If you are going to permit pets, you may want to consider requiring an added month's deposit, specifying a place for defecation by the pet, and requiring the tenant to pay for professional carpet shampooing on leaving.

Other Items Not Covered in the Sample Lease

Use of Outdoor Space: In the rules attached to your lease, you should consider defining what outdoor space, if any, you will permit your tenant to use, and under what conditions.

Access to Fuses: Unless you are certain that you will be in your house all the time, or unless utilities are completely separated, you will have to deal with the problem of giving the tenant access to electrical fuses or circuit breakers. This access should be defined in the rules attached to the lease, and instructions should be posted on how to change fuses or rethrow circuit breakers.

Service Exchanges: Any agreement on service exchanges should be incorporated into the body of the lease by reference. For an example of how this is done, see the section in the sample lease on tenant obligations.

CONCLUSION

Finding a tenant is the last major step. When the apartment is installed, and the tenant has moved in, you should have a sense of accomplishment. You should also begin to feel the benefits of the apartment in your pocketbook, or in your sense of security, or in your satisfaction that a parent or child is living close to you.

At this point, if you have just finished this book, but have not yet begun the process of installing the apartment, the process may seem overwhelming. In the effort to be comprehensive, we may have provided too much material and made the process of installing the apartment seem worse than it is. Don't be overwhelmed. As we have pointed out earlier, there are people who can help you in each stage of the process. The task of this book is to help you avoid mistakes. As a result, it necessarily overemphasizes problems. They are real but avoidable. This book should help you avoid them. Many you would probably avoid anyway out of common sense. If the problems were truly enormous, there would not be so many accessory apartments around.

This book should also help you get all the benefits you can from having an apartment: income, added security, companionship if you want it, and a source of inexpensive services provided in return for rent reductions. If you have doubts, work through the pro forma in Appendix 10. Apply it to your own situation, but put in additional figures: Add in a dollar value for the cost to you of the problems of installing the apartment; add in the dollar benefit of the extra security you will have; and so forth.

Make sure an accessory apartment will work for you. And good luck.

APPENDIX 1

COMPENSATION FOR SERVICES

Law

The applicable sections of the Internal Revenue Code of 1954 and the Income Tax Regulations thereunder are 61(a) and 1.61-2, relating to compensation for services.

Section 1.61-2(d)(1) of the regulations provides that if services are paid for other than in money, the fair market value of the property or services taken in payment must be included in income. If the services were rendered at a stipulated price, such price will be presumed to be the fair market value of the compensation received in the absence of evidence to the contrary.

Situation

An individual who owned an apartment building received a work of art created by a professional artist in return for the rent-free use of an apartment for six months by the artist.

The fair market value of the work of art and the six months fair rental value of the apartment are includible in the gross income of the apartment-owner and the artist under section 61 of the Code.

Internal Revenue Cumulative Bulletin 7901, pp. 60–61.

APPENDIX 2

RENTING PART OF
YOUR PROPERTY

If you rent part of your property and use the other part for personal purposes, you must divide your basis for depreciation between the rental part and the personal part.

Example

You paid $60,000 for your home, of which $12,000 was for the land and $48,000 was for the building. You live in half of the house and rent out the other half. The basis you use for depreciation on the rental part is $24,000 ($\frac{1}{2} \times$ $48,000).

Internal Revenue Service Publication No. 527, *Rental Property*, p. 5.

APPENDIX 3

PROPERTY CHANGED TO RENTAL USE

When you hold property for personal use and change it to rental use, such as renting your former home, your basis for depreciation is the smaller of

1. The fair market value of the property at the date of change, or
2. Your adjusted basis of the property at the date of the change. Your adjusted basis is your original cost or other basis of the property plus the cost of improvements or additions you made since you got the property and minus deductions for casualty losses claimed on earlier years' income tax returns and other charges to basis.

Example

You paid $60,000 for a home several years ago when a fair division of the cost was $10,000 for the land and $50,000 for the house. Shortly after buying the property, you added a second story to the house at a cost of $17,600 and a patio at a cost of $2,400. After these additions, your adjusted basis of the house was $70,000.

Last year you began renting out the second floor of your home, two bedrooms and a bath. This was three-sevenths of your house. The total fair market value of the property at the date of the change to rental use was $90,000. The land had appreciated to a value of $16,000, so that the value of the house when you began renting out a part of it was $74,000.

Because the fair market value of the house at the time of the change to rental use ($74,000) was more than your adjusted basis at that time ($70,000), you must use $70,000, the smaller of the two, to figure your basis for depreciation. Because three-sevenths of the total area of your house was changed to rental use, $30,000 ($3/7 \times $70,000) is your basis for depreciation.

Internal Revenue Service Publication No. 527, *Rental Property*, p. 5.

APPENDIX 4

USEFUL LIFE

You must determine the useful life of depreciable property placed in service before 1981 or property that does not qualify for the ACRS method. The useful life of an asset depends on how long you expect to use it; its age when you got it; your policy as to repairs, upkeep, and replacement; and other conditions.

There is no average useful life that applies in all situations. It is determined on the basis of your particular operating conditions, experience, and replacement policy. The useful life is not necessarily the life of the asset, but is the period over which you reasonably expect to use the asset. If your experience is inadequate, you may use the general experience of other owners of similar rental property until your own experience is adequate.

You must determine the useful life of your property, such as a building or furniture, by using all available facts at the time you begin using the property for rental purposes. The materials used in construction and the age and condition of the house or other property when bought or changed to rental use are factors you should consider in determining the useful life of the property. A new, well-constructed brick home may have a life of 50 years or more, whereas a frame house that is not as well constructed may have a life of 25 years or less.

Internal Revenue Service Publication No. 527, *Rental Property*, p. 4.

APPENDIX 5

SALVAGE VALUE

You may have to consider the salvage value of property that does not qualify for the ACRS method when you figure your yearly depreciation deduction.

The salvage value of your rental property, such as a house, furniture, or appliances, is the part of the expected selling price at the end of the property's useful life that would be for the rental part. You determine salvage value when you get the rental property or when you change your property to rental use. You may not change it later because of price level changes.

Net salvage is salvage reduced by the cost of removing the property. You may use either salvage or net salvage in figuring depreciation, but you must use one of them consistently. However, you may not use negative net salvage. The net salvage is zero when the expected costs of removal are more than the expected salvage value. If you refigure the useful life of an asset, you should refigure the salvage value at the same time.

Personal Property

You may reduce the salvage value of personal property with a useful life of three years or more by up to 10% of the basis of the property. If salvage value is less than 10% of your basis, you may disregard it.

Internal Revenue Service Publication No. 527, *Rental Property*, p. 5.

15-, 18-, & 19-YEAR ACRS TABLES

15-year Real Property (other than low-income housing)

Year	Month Placed in Service											
	1	2	3	4	5	6	7	8	9	10	11	12
1st	12%	11%	10%	9%	8%	7%	6%	5%	4%	3%	2%	1%
2d	10%	10%	11%	11%	11%	11%	11%	11%	11%	11%	11%	12%
3d	9%	9%	9%	9%	10%	10%	10%	10%	10%	10%	10%	10%
4th	8%	8%	8%	8%	8%	8%	9%	9%	9%	9%	9%	9%
5th	7%	7%	7%	7%	7%	7%	8%	8%	8%	8%	8%	8%
6th	6%	6%	6%	6%	7%	7%	7%	7%	7%	7%	7%	7%
7th	6%	6%	6%	6%	6%	6%	6%	6%	6%	6%	6%	6%
8th	6%	6%	6%	6%	6%	6%	5%	6%	6%	6%	6%	6%
9th	6%	6%	6%	6%	5%	6%	5%	5%	5%	6%	6%	6%
10th	5%	6%	5%	6%	5%	5%	5%	5%	5%	5%	6%	5%
11th	5%	5%	5%	5%	5%	5%	5%	5%	5%	5%	5%	5%
12th	5%	5%	5%	5%	5%	5%	5%	5%	5%	5%	5%	5%
13th	5%	5%	5%	5%	5%	5%	5%	5%	5%	5%	5%	5%
14th	5%	5%	5%	5%	5%	5%	5%	5%	5%	5%	5%	5%
15th	5%	5%	5%	5%	5%	5%	5%	5%	5%	5%	5%	5%
16th	—	—	1%	1%	2%	2%	3%	3%	4%	4%	4%	5%

18-year Real Property
(placed in service after March 15 and before June 23, 1984)

Year	Month Placed in Service										
	1	2	3	4	5	6	7	8	9	10–11	12
1st	10%	9%	8%	7%	6%	6%	5%	4%	3%	2%	1%
2nd	9%	9%	9%	9%	9%	9%	9%	9%	9%	10%	10%
3rd	8%	8%	8%	8%	8%	8%	8%	8%	9%	9%	9%
4th	7%	7%	7%	7%	7%	7%	8%	8%	8%	8%	8%
5th	6%	7%	7%	7%	7%	7%	7%	7%	7%	7%	7%
6th	6%	6%	6%	6%	6%	6%	6%	6%	6%	6%	6%
7th	5%	5%	5%	5%	6%	6%	6%	6%	6%	6%	6%
8–12th	5%	5%	5%	5%	5%	5%	5%	5%	5%	5%	5%
13th	4%	4%	4%	5%	5%	4%	4%	5%	4%	4%	4%
14–18th	4%	4%	4%	4%	4%	4%	4%	4%	4%	4%	4%
19th			1%	1%	1%	2%	2%	2%	3%	3%	4%

18-year Real Property
(placed in service after June 22, 1984)

Year	Month Placed in Service											
	1	2	3	4	5	6	7	8	9	10	11	12
1st	9%	9%	8%	7%	6%	5%	4%	4%	3%	2%	1%	0.4%
2nd	9%	9%	9%	9%	9%	9%	9%	9%	9%	10%	10%	10%
3rd	8%	8%	8%	8%	8%	8%	8%	8%	9%	9%	9%	9%
4th	7%	7%	7%	7%	7%	8%	8%	8%	8%	8%	8%	8%
5th	7%	7%	7%	7%	7%	7%	7%	7%	7%	7%	7%	7%
6th	6%	6%	6%	6%	6%	6%	6%	6%	6%	6%	6%	6%
7th	5%	5%	5%	5%	6%	6%	6%	6%	6%	6%	6%	6%
8–12th	5%	5%	5%	5%	5%	5%	5%	5%	5%	5%	5%	5%
13th	4%	4%	4%	5%	4%	4%	5%	4%	4%	4%	5%	5%
14–17th	4%	4%	4%	4%	4%	4%	4%	4%	4%	4%	4%	4%
18th	4%	3%	4%	4%	4%	4%	4%	4%	4%	4%	4%	4%
19th			1%	1%	1%	2%	2%	2%	3%	3%	3%	3.6%

19-year Real Property

Year	Month Placed in Service											
	1	2	3	4	5	6	7	8	9	10	11	12
1st	8.8	8.1	7.3	6.5	5.8	5.0	4.2	3.5	2.7	1.9	1.1	0.4
2nd	8.4	8.5	8.5	8.6	8.7	8.8	8.8	8.9	9.0	9.0	9.1	9.2
3rd	7.6	7.7	7.7	7.8	7.9	7.9	8.0	8.1	8.1	8.2	8.3	8.3
4th	6.9	7.0	7.0	7.1	7.1	7.2	7.3	7.3	7.4	7.4	7.5	7.6
5th	6.3	6.3	6.4	6.4	6.5	6.5	6.6	6.6	6.7	6.8	6.8	6.9
6th	5.7	5.7	5.8	5.9	5.9	5.9	6.0	6.0	6.1	6.1	6.2	6.2
7th	5.2	5.2	5.3	5.3	5.3	5.4	5.4	5.5	5.5	5.6	5.6	5.6
8th	4.7	4.7	4.8	4.8	4.8	4.9	4.9	5.0	5.0	5.1	5.1	5.1
9th	4.2	4.3	4.3	4.4	4.4	4.5	4.5	4.5	4.5	4.6	4.6	4.7
10–19th	4.2	4.2	4.2	4.2	4.2	4.2	4.2	4.2	4.2	4.2	4.2	4.2
20th	0.2	0.5	0.9	1.2	1.6	1.9	2.3	2.6	3.0	3.3	3.7	4.0

Internal Revenue Service Publication No. 527, *Rental Property*, p. 3.

APPENDIX 7

IRS SCHEDULE E: SUPPLEMENTAL INCOME SCHEDULE

SCHEDULE E (Form 1040)	**Supplemental Income Schedule**	OMB No. 1545-0074
Department of the Treasury Internal Revenue Service (O)	(From rents and royalties, partnerships, estates, and trusts, etc.) ▶ Attach to Form 1040. ▶ See Instructions for Schedule E (Form 1040).	19**85** 13
Name(s) as shown on Form 1040		Your social security number

Part I Rental and Royalty Income or Loss

1 In the space provided below, show the kind and location of each rental property.

2 For each property listed, did you or a member of your family use for personal purposes any of the properties for more than the greater of 14 days or 10% of the total days rented at fair rental value during the tax year?   Yes   No

Property A...▶
Property B...▶
Property C...▶

Rental and Royalty Income		Properties			Totals (Add columns A, B, and C)
		A	B	C	
3 a Rents received					} 3
b Royalties received					
Rental and Royalty Expenses					
4 Advertising	4				
5 Auto and travel	5				
6 Cleaning and maintenance	6				
7 Commissions	7				
8 Insurance	8				
9 Legal and other professional fees	9				
10 Mortgage interest paid to financial institutions (see Instructions)	10				10
11 Other interest	11				
12 Repairs	12				
13 Supplies	13				
14 Taxes (Do **not** include Windfall Profit Tax here. See Part III, line 34.)	14				
15 Utilities	15				
16 Wages and salaries	16				
17 Other (list) ▶					
....					
....					
....					
....					
....					
....					
....					
....					
18 Total expenses other than depreciation and depletion. Add lines 4 through 17	18				18
19 Depreciation expense (see Part V Instructions), or depletion	19				19
20 Total. Add lines 18 and 19	20				
21 Income or (loss) from rental or royalty properties. Subtract line 20 from line 3a (rents) or 3b (royalties)	21				

22 Add properties with profits on line 21, and write the total profits here 22

23 Add properties with losses on line 21, and write the total (losses) here . . . . 23 ( )

24 Combine amounts on lines 22 and 23, and write the net profit or (loss) here 24

25 Net farm rental profit or (loss) from Form 4835, line 35 25

26 Total rental or royalty income or (loss). Combine amounts on lines 24 and 25, and write the total here. If Parts II and III on page 2 do not apply to you, write the amount from line 26 on Form 1040, line 18. Otherwise, include the amount in line 36 on page 2 of Schedule E 26

For Paperwork Reduction Act Notice, see Form 1040 Instructions.   Schedule E (Form 1040) 1985

APPENDIX 8

IRS FORM 4562: DEPRECIATION AND AMORTIZATION

Form **4562**	**Depreciation and Amortization**	OMB No. 1545-0172
Department of the Treasury Internal Revenue Service	▶ See separate instructions. ▶ Attach this form to your return.	19**85** 67
Name(s) as shown on return		Identifying number

Business or activity to which this form relates

Part I Depreciation
Use Part III, Specific Information Concerning Automobiles and other Listed Property, for certain transportation equipment (e.g. autos), amusement/recreation property, and computer/peripheral equipment.

Section A.—Election to Expense Recovery Property (Section 179)

(a) Class of property	(b) Cost	(c) Expense deduction
1		

2 Listed property—Enter total from Part III, Section A, column (h) . . . .

3 Total (see instructions for limitations). (Partnerships or S corporations—see the Schedule K and Schedule K-1 Instructions of Form 1065 or 1120S) . . . .

Section B.—Depreciation of Recovery Property

(a) Class of property	(b) Date placed in service	(c) Cost or other basis	(d) Recovery period	(e) Method of figuring depreciation	(f) Deduction
4 Accelerated Cost Recovery System (ACRS) (see instructions): *For assets other than automobiles and other listed property placed in service* **ONLY** *during tax year beginning in 1985*					
a 3-year property					
b 5-year property					
c 10-year property					
d 15-year public utility property					
e Low-income housing					
f 15-year real property					
g 18-year real property					
(See "Items You Should Note")					

5 Listed property—Enter total from Part III, Section A, column (g) . . . .

6 ACRS deduction for assets other than automobiles and other listed property placed in service prior to 1985 (see instructions) . . . .

Section C.—Depreciation of Nonrecovery Property

7 Property subject to section 168(e)(2) election (see instructions) . . . .

8 Other depreciation (see instructions) . . . .

Section D.—Summary

9 Total (Add deductions on lines 3 through 8). Enter here and on the Depreciation line of your return (Partnerships and S corporations—Do NOT include any amounts entered on line 3.) . . . .

Part II Amortization

(a) Description of property	(b) Date acquired	(c) Cost or other basis	(d) Code section	(e) Amortization period or percentage	(f) Amortization for this year
		·			

Total. Enter here and on Other Deductions or Other Expenses line of your return . . . .

See Paperwork Reduction Act Notice on page 1 of the separate instructions.   Form **4562** (1985)

APPENDIX 9

FIVE STEPS FOR OBTAINING HUD HOME IMPROVEMENT LOANS

1. Discuss the proposed job with the customer. Describe in detail the work to be done. Compute the total cost of the job. Then, using the gross-charge table, tell the customer the term of the note, the amount of the financing charge, and the amount of the monthly payments necessary to pay off the loan. If the work is agreed upon, prepare a detailed written contract or sales agreement in at least three copies—one for yourself, one for the customer, and one for the lending institution. This contract or sales agreement must be properly dated, and signed by both the customer and the dealer or contractor. Be sure that the wording of the contract specifies (1) the type of improvements, (2) the extent of the improvements, and (3) a description of the materials to be used.

2. Have the customer fill out and sign a credit application, carefully, completely, and accurately.

3. Deliver the completed credit application and a copy of the contract to the lending institution. If your customer's credit

228

is acceptable, the lending institution will notify both you and the customer.

4. After receiving notice of the acceptability of the customer's credit, do the job called for in the contract in a businesslike manner. When the work is completed according to the agreement and to the customer's satisfaction, see that the completion certificate is properly dated, properly filled in, and properly signed by both the customer and the dealer or contractor. Remember:

   - The completion certificate must be dated the day it is signed by the borrowers.

   - Borrowers must sign it only *after* work has been completed.

   - The dealer, contractor, or an authorized agent must sign the certificate.

   - The certificate warrants that the dealer-contractor will repurchase the note if any representations made on the dealer-contractor portion of the form prove incorrect.

5. The lending institution pays the dealer or contractor the net proceeds of the loan, provided at least six days have elapsed since the customer was notified of the acceptability of the application.

From "Dealer and Contractor Guide to Property Improvement Loans," U.S. Department of Housing and Urban Development.

APPENDIX 10

PRO FORMA FOR AN
ACCESSORY APARTMENT

Situation: Older home in Fairfax County, Virginia, to be occupied by widowed homeowner and tenant(s)[1]

Square footage: Total, 1,500; accessory apartment, 500 square feet, or 33 percent[2]

Basis for depreciation:[3]

Original purchase price	$60,000
Less value of land (20%)	− 12,000
	48,000
Less 67% of house not used for apartment	− 32,160
	15,840
Plus $10,000 improvement from installing apartment	+ 10,000
	$25,840

Tax Deductions[4]

Depreciation[5] (15-year straight-line method)	$1,723
Real estate tax deduction increase[6]	147
Interest on loan to install apartment[7] (first year)	1,466
Expenses[8] (heat, electricity, water and sewer, repairs)	1,109
Total Deductions	**$4,445**

Net Change in Homeowner's Annual Income

Value of rental income and tenant's services[9] ($3,600 rental income + $1,200 tenant's services)	$4,800
Tax deductions with apartment[10] ($4,445 × 20%)	+889
Payments on loan to install apartment[7] ($161.33 × 12)	−1,936
Total Net Change	**+$3,753**[11]

Assumptions and Sources for Pro Forma

1. This is an older home in Fairfax County, Virginia, that will be occupied by the widowed homeowner and a tenant in an accessory apartment. The tenant moved in on January 1, the beginning of the tax year, so all computations are based on a 12-month period.

2. The total square footage of the house is 1,500. The apartment is 500 square feet or 33 percent of the total area. Therefore, 33 percent is used as the basis for deductions such as heat and electricity.

3. The original purchase price of the home was $60,000. Value of the lot is assumed to be 20 percent of the original purchase price, or $12,000. Only that portion of the house used by the tenant may be used for depreciation, so the homeowner's portion of the house, 67 percent, is also deducted. The owner invested $10,000 to install the apartment, which results in a total basis for depreciation of

$25,840. The fair market value of the house after installation of the apartment is $110,000.

4. Based on Internal Revenue Service Publication No. 527, *Rental Property*, 1981.

5. Straight-line depreciation over a 15-year period was used, rather than the accelerated cost recovery system, because the house was owned prior to 1981.

6. Real estate taxes in Fairfax County in 1982 were levied at the rate of $1.47 per $100.00 of assessed value. Theoretically, the house was assessed at $100,000 before the installation of the accessory apartment, with an annual tax bill of $1,470. The $10,000 addition would raise the bill to $147.

7. There is no longer a first mortgage on the house. The owner borrowed $10,000 to install the apartment. Assuming a 15 percent loan for 10 years, monthly payments at $161.33 amount to $1,936 per year.

8. Increases in expenses for the tenant are relatively small (10 or 20 percent) since most utilities and repairs would be required whether or not the tenant were present.

	Prior to Apartment	Including Tenant	33% Attributable to Apartment
Heat[a]	$1,200	$1,320 (10%)	$436
Electricity[b]	600	720 (20%)	238
Water and sewer[c]	200	240 (20%)	79
Repairs[d]	900	1,080 (20%)	356

a. Washington Gas Light Company, telephone conversation, September 22, 1982. $1,200 quoted as yearly consumption for gas heat in large older home. This amount was used as the basis for the gas company's budget plan for larger older homes in 1981.

b. Virginia Electric Power Company, telephone conversation, September 22, 1982. $600 quoted for yearly consumption of electricity assuming two people in the household, nonelectric heat, and electric air conditioning.

c. Fairfax County Water Authority, telephone conversation, September 22, 1982. $200 quoted as average annual water and sewer bill for two-person household.

d. Repairs are conservatively estimated at $900 based on experience of managing large older houses from 1977–1982. This figure includes some painting, cleaning gutters, replacing broken windows, fixing locks, patching plaster, etc. Figure will vary from house to house depending on conditions.

9. $300 per month for apartment rental is a very conservative figure for the Washington, D.C., area. Fair market rental value of the unit is easily $400. Assume that the tenant agrees that in exchange for the lower rent, he or she will maintain the yard and provide two hours of transportation to the homeowner each week. Technically, these services, valued at $100 per month, should be reported to the IRS as income. However, it seems unlikely the discrepancy would become apparent.

10. Homeowner is assumed to be in the 20 percent bracket. Since the mortgage was paid off prior to installation of apartment, homeowner's only deduction has been real estate taxes. See note 6 for derivation of taxes.

11. This is the net change in annual income, assuming that the homeowner has enough taxable income to need deductions.

APPENDIX 11

ACCESSORY APARTMENT PRECHECK—Honolulu, Hawaii

OHANA DWELLING
Public Facilities Precheck

			TAX MAP KEY	
Zone	Sec.	Plat	Par.	Lot No.

OWNER'S NAME   (Please Print/Type)

Phone Number _____

ADDRESS

APPLICANT'S NAME

Phone Number: _____

ADDRESS

★ ★ ★ ★ ★ ★ ★ ★ ★ ★ ★ ★ ★ ★ ★ ★ INSTRUCTIONS FOR COMPLETING FORM ★ ★ ★ ★ ★ ★ ★ ★ ★ ★ ★ ★ ★ ★ ★ ★

1. Applicant must provide all information in Section I.
2. Applicant must acquire approvals and signatures from all four agencies as listed in Section II. If any one agency does not approve, a Bldg. Permit cannot be granted.
3. Submit approved form along with Bldg. Permit application and required drawings to the Bldg. Dept

★ ★

SECTION I.

1. PROPOSAL FOR: (Check one)
   _____One additional unit
   _____Two new units (vacant lot)
   _____Use of existing second unit
   _____Converting 1-family unit to 2-family
          (Interior work only)
2. NUMBER OF NEW/ADDED BEDROOMS_____
3. PARCEL NOW SERVED BY OR HAS: (Check Yes Or No)
   a. Municipal sewers or private treatment works (not cesspool/septic tank).   _____YES _____NO
   b. Direct access to a street with minimum paved roadway width of 16 feet.   _____YES _____NO

   PROCEED TO SECTION II Only If The Above Items Are Checked Yes

★ ★

SECTION II.
STEP

1. BUILDING DEPT., 1st Flr., Municipal Bldg., 650 So. King St., Permit Section 523-4505
   Parcel is zoned residential.
   _____YES
   _____NO   CHECKED BY: _____   _____
                                          SIGNATURE   DATE
2. FIRE DEPT., 1st Flr., Municipal Bldg. in Bldg. Dept., 650 So. King St., 523-4186
   Street/roadway meets access requirements.
   _____YES
   _____NO   CHECKED BY: _____   _____
                                          SIGNATURE   DATE
3. DEPT. OF PUBLIC WORKS, Div. of Wastewater Management, Public Service Section,
   650 So. King St., 523-4429
   a. Property presently served by: ____Municipal Sewer ____Private Sewer ____Cesspool/Septic Tank
   b. Existing municipal sewer system is: ____Adequate ____Inadequate

           CHECKED BY: _____   _____
                                          SIGNATURE   DATE
4. BOARD OF WATER SUPPLY (across street from Municipal Bldg. parking garage), Service Engineering Section, Ground
   Flr., 630 So. Beretania St., 548-6189 or 6190.
   _____APPROVED
   _____DENIED   CHECKED BY: _____   _____
                                          SIGNATURE   DATE

★★★★★★★★★★★★★★THIS FORM IS NOT PERMISSION TO BUILD AND ALL OTHER REQUIREMENTS OF LAW MUST BE
MET.   THIS FORM EXPIRES 90 DAYS AFTER BOARD OF WATER SUPPLY CLEARANCE DATE.★★★★★★★★★★★★★★

Note: Compliance with private covenants or lease restrictions prohibiting two dwelling units on a lot is applicant's responsibility.

234

HOW TO APPLY
FOR A BUILDING PERMIT—
Honolulu, Hawaii

If your precheck form is signed and approved by all four (4) agencies, then you may submit final construction plans for a building permit. *Your precheck form expires ninety (90) days after Board of Water Supply approval.*

The following is a general description of the requirements for a building permit:

Building Permits Are Required

1. To erect, construct, alter, remove, or demolish any building or structure (including fences, retaining walls and swimming pools).

2. For any electrical or plumbing work.

3. To construct or alter any sidewalk, curb or driveway in public rights-of-way.

What to Bring

Three (3) sets of plans and a completed building permit application.

Architect's/Engineer's Seal

Plans must be properly stamped and signed by an architect or structural engineer, if the principal structural members are of reinforced concrete or structural steel regardless of value.

Plans must be properly stamped and signed by an architect, structural engineer, or civil engineer for retaining walls five (5) feet or more in height.

Permit Fee

The minimum fee is $6.00 for work up to $500 in value. This fee increases as the value of the work being done increases.

Information to Be Provided on Plans

1. On plot plan, show lot dimensions, location of driveway, location of proposed work, distance from property lines and other buildings, easements and other pertinent information. Plans should be drawn to scale with sufficient information and details to clearly show the nature and extent of work.
2. On floor plan, indicate the use of rooms, room dimensions, location and sizes of windows, exits, etc.
3. On framing plans or typical section view, show sizes and spacing of beams, floor joists, rafters, etc., and ceiling heights.
4. On outside or exterior elevation views, show height of building and existing and finished grades.
5. Give address and/or tax map key of where the work is to be done, and the name and address of owner.
6. Give name and address of person who prepared plans (if other than owner).

INDEX